N

Ninety Seconds to Tell It All
Big Business and the News Media

NINETY SECONDS TO TELL IT ALL
Big Business and the News Media

A. Kent MacDougall

DOW JONES-IRWIN
Homewood, Illinois 60430

ISBN 0-87094-268-9
Library of Congress Catalog Card No. 81-67970

Printed in the United States of America

1 2 3 4 5 6 7 8 9 0 K 8 7 6 5 4 3 2 1

Contents

Introduction

Whenever business executives get together and start swapping stories about the beating they think they've taken from ignorant, ill-willed journalists, someone is sure to bring up the *New York Times* front page story that reported—erroneously—that the oil industry had deliberately worsened the oil shortage. Or the *Washington Post* front page story that broke the confidentiality of a federal report on "problem" banks. Or the *Los Angeles Times* cartoon that likened DC-10 jetliners to the ill-fated *Titanic.*

For the most flagrant examples of accusatory, distorted coverage, however, the business executives are likely to turn to television. Someone is sure to bring up the investigative reporter for "NBC Nightly News" who was caught ignoring evidence that would have weakened his case against an oil company. Or the combative correspondent for CBS's "60 Minutes" who practiced selective quotesmanship to make a document appear more damaging to a chemical company. Or the ABC documentary on uranium mining that passed off vented water vapor as deadly radon gas.

Many a business executive can cite a run-in with a naive reporter who demonstrated by his questioning or his story that he didn't know the difference between a stock and a bond, much less how to read a balance sheet or understand the complexities of interest rates. And many a business executive can go on at length about how journalists are giving profits a dirty name, exaggerating environmental hazards, sensationalizing marketplace rip-offs, and sowing public distrust of business at a time when the capitalist system is under increasing strain and needs the media's understanding and support more than ever.

Discord between businessmen and journalists is nothing new, of course. But it wasn't until the early 1970s that business accusations of ignorant, distorted, negative, biased coverage of business became commonplace. Watergate had a lot to do with it. Many businessmen blamed the news media for ganging up on President Richard M. Nixon and helping drive him from office. And many thought that the press's distrust of the Nixon Administration was spilling over and jaundicing journalists' attitude toward business and other powerful institutions.

Whether or not journalists were guilty of an anti-Establishment "post-Watergate mentality" that colored their coverage, it was actually a corporate crime wave that caused much of the bad press business received. No fewer than 117 of the largest and most prestigious U.S. corporations were convicted of federal offenses during the 1970s, or made settlements, according to a survey by *Fortune* magazine. And the *Fortune* survey was limited to just five domestic offenses—criminal antitrust violations, bribery and kickbacks, illegal political contributions, criminal fraud, and tax evasion. *Fortune* said the list would have been longer had it included foreign bribes and kickbacks.

Besides the series of scandals that plagued business starting in 1973, there was the dollar crisis, the energy crisis, and other signs of fundamental problems with the U.S. economy. Business's stock sank not just with journalists but with the public. And that's about when top business executives started counterattacking. In public speeches and guest newspaper columns, top executives of Bethlehem Steel Corporation, Prudential Insurance Company, Citicorp, General Foods Corporation, Norton Simon Inc., and other major corporations vented their resentment. Typical was the warning by David J. Mahoney, chairman and president of Norton Simon, that businessmen were no longer "going to suffer silently while being blamed for the sins of the world by self-styled adversaries who substitute trendy distrust for objective standards of accountability."

Even news media executives joined the griping. Said Katharine Graham, chairman of the Washington Post Company: "I, too, have felt victimized by headlines such as those proclaiming that profits are up 50 percent when profit margins rose from 2 percent to 3 percent. I have been angered by reporting on labor disputes, production problems, and Equal Employment Opportunity complaints when stories failed to reflect what I thought were important factors or constraints on management."

Louis Banks, a former managing editor of *Fortune* who went on to teach at the Harvard Business School, also took business's side. In an article in the *Atlantic Monthly*, "Memo to the Press: They

Hate You Out There," Banks likened ignorant business reporters to "kids with loaded pistols prowling through the forests of corporate complexity to play games of cowboys and Indians or good guys and bad guys. Their only interest in business is to find a negative story that will get them promoted out of business into Woodward and Bernstein."

Banks was correct in suggesting that the media had a built-in bias in favor of negative news. Negative news not only sells newspapers, but it calls attention to problems that require correction and thus strikes journalists as more important than positive news about things that are going right and can take care of themselves. But Banks was off-base in suggesting there were a lot of ignorant business reporters out gunning for business. A handful of investigative reporters scattered throughout the country may have been delightedly digging up dirt on business. But the overwhelming majority of business reporters, the sophisticated as well as the ignorant, were so bogged down covering routine business news against daily deadlines that they had no time, much less the inclination, to ambush business.

If too many business reporters had too little idea of how business worked, businessmen had little idea of the different ways in which the divergent media operated. Wire service reporters sent out on assignments unprepared to understand the complexities they were expected to report on in a hurry had little in common with writers for *Fortune* with several months to research a single article. And the scarcity of time on network evening newscasts to treat any story adequately bore little relation to the situation on newspapers with business pages to fill each day.

Journalists didn't like taking the blame for the bad news they reported but did not create. They denied they were antibusiness, saying they were just anti-bad business. They didn't agree that going beyond corporate news releases constituted giving business the business. And they were sick of businessmen reacting defensively to even the most thoroughly researched and evenly balanced accounts.

And when it came to horror stories, the journalists had some of their own. They could cite the deceptive news releases that Bank of America issued to try to cover up the dismissal of a senior executive. Or Pacific Gas & Electric Company's attempt to discredit a television newsman by falsely accusing him of tampering with an interview. Or the pharmaceutical manufacturers that retaliated for a *New York Times* series on inept medical practices and adverse drug reactions by withdrawing $500,000 in advertising from a *Times*-owned medical magazine.

As the charges and countercharges flew and animosity between businessmen and journalists intensified, it became clear it was time for an in-depth, dispassionate examination of how businessmen disseminate news and how journalists gather and present it. John F. Lawrence, assistant managing editor of the *Los Angeles Times* for economic affairs, decided that the *Los Angeles Times* ought to undertake the definitive business-media study. He assigned the project to me.

To make the study manageable, I concentrated on how major metropolitan newspapers and the three commercial television networks cover business. I solicited complaints from scores of major corporations and business trade associations, examined these complaints and matched them against the media's performance. I also looked into the flood of free product plugs and unlabeled corporate advocacy that business manages to get into newspapers and onto television in the guise of legitimate news and features.

My business-media study took a year and a half and resulted in a nine-part series of articles in the *Los Angeles Times*. This book is based on that series. Besides conceiving the series, my editor, John Lawrence, made countless suggestions that improved the final product and showed support throughout. My wife and editor of first resort, Kathleen D. MacDougall, read all my drafts, saving me from many infelicities in logic and language. And my father, Curtis D. MacDougall, set the high standards of critical analysis and scholarly discipline I have used as a model in all my work.

1

Holding Business Accountable

Businessmen who rank journalists with bureaucrats and environmentalists as their most irksome tormentors began about 1979 to strike back at newspaper and television news coverage they considered biased against them.

In Des Moines, Iowa, two dozen business leaders signed a statement accusing the *Des Moines Register* of unbalanced, unfair, and cynical coverage for, among other things, reporting corporate executives' salaries and even problems with alcoholism. Oil companies started getting back for what they considered inexpert, inaccurate, and even accusatory coverage on network television. Mobil Corporation took two-page ads in a dozen newspapers to denounce a "biased" and "shoddy" report on oil company profits on CBS-TV. And Exxon Corporation and Shell Oil Company filed complaints over unflattering coverage on NBC-TV with the National News Council, an independent group that monitors media performance.

Some companies haled journalists into court. Bristol-Myers Company sued CBS for $25 million

over a report on the network's New York television
station that questioned advertised claims for
Bufferin and Excedrin pain relievers. American
Family Life Assurance Company slapped a $275
million libel suit against ABC–TV for using hidden
cameras and other investigative methods to prepare
a "deliberately distorted, perverted, and staged"
story on cancer insurance. And William P. Tavoulareas, president of Mobil, filed a $100 million libel
suit against the *Washington Post*, charging it had
printed false reports that he had improperly set up
his son Peter in the shipping business.

Hints of economic reprisal rent the air. Leonard
S. Matthews, president of the American Association of Advertising Agencies, warned that TV
journalists could not expect business to continue
supporting a medium that stereotypes it as "greedy,
insensitive, and antisocial."

Business complaints prompted some news organizations to pull in their journalistic horns. A number of newspapers and TV stations fired or reas-
signed reporters and editors who had offended
advertisers and other business interests. *The Dan-
bury* (Conn.) *News-Times* discharged an editor for
publishing a photograph of the owner of a "lemon"
picketing a local Ford auto agency, explaining he
had failed to include the agency's side of the story.
And NBC's television station in Chicago, WMAQ,
fired consumer affairs reporter Roberta Baskin—it
said for advocating consumerist positions without
giving business its fair say, she said because she had
stepped on too many businessmen's toes.

The number of full-time consumer reporters in
the nation's news media fell from a peak of 500 in
1974 to 200 by 1980, Francis Pollock, former

editor of *Media & Consumer* magazine, estimated. And many consumer reporters who survived concentrated on snappy, inoffensive superficialities rather than significant exposés of consumer rip-offs.

As the decline in consumer reporting indicates, the public has a stake in the controversy between business and the press. If the news media are really giving business a hard time, they may be undermining the public and governmental support business needs to thrive and spur the economy. On the other hand, if what Americans don't know can harm them, any fall-off in news media scrutiny of business practices and malpractices reduces the effectiveness of the early warning system that the press provides in alerting the public and the government to business abuses that require correction.

Ironically, the business–press controversy began heating up at a time when some captains of industry and commerce who were early, vocal critics of business news coverage were crediting journalists with increasing competence, sophistication and fairness. The critics could take some of the credit, for major news organizations had responded to the criticism, as well as to the increasing importance of of business and economic developments, by bolstering their business news staffs and expanding and upgrading their coverage. For instance, the TV networks added specialists in business and economic news who usually, if not always, gave businessmen their say.

As this study documents, there is considerable evidence to support business complaints that media coverage is often simplistic, careless and cursory. But cases of deliberate distortion remain rare. At the same time, there are indications that business enjoys a much more sympathetic press than it generally acknowledges. Not only do editorial writers generally endorse business positions, but newspapers publish a considerable amount of fluff supplied by businesses to promote food, fashions, travel, real estate, sports, and stocks. And many smaller papers and TV and radio stations use, often without attribution to the source, business-supplied canned editorials, columns, and features that grind industry's ax and polish its image.

Polishing industry's image has grown increasingly urgent as business has fallen in the public's esteem. Whereas 70 percent of Americans polled by Yankelovich, Skelly & White in 1968 believed that business tries for a fair balance between profits and the interests of the public, only 19 percent did so in 1979. And according to Louis Harris polls, Americans expressing a great deal of confidence in the people running major companies fell from 55 percent in 1966 to 16 percent in 1980.

Businessmen pin much of the blame for rising mistrust of business on the government and the media. Of business executives polled in 1979 by Yankelovich, Skelly & White, 41 percent said the government was primarily responsible for antibusiness sentiment, while 24 percent blamed the media and 35 percent blamed business itself.

It's hard to find an oil industry executive who doesn't hold the news media largely responsible for the public's belief that oil companies concocted the energy shortage to justify higher fuel prices and reap windfall profits. Among other sins, the oil men say, the press has provided a forum for the charges of irresponsible politicians who have manipulated the energy issue for their own political advantage.

Of course, many of the politicians who have made what the oil industry calls irresponsible statements are high officials of the federal government, whose policies and actions could hardly be ignored by an alert and self-respecting press. Indeed, the government has initiated much of the negative business news of recent years, with a seemingly unending flow of revelations about businesses that pollute rivers, poison workers, produce dangerous products, rig prices, monopolize markets, doctor the books, bribe foreign government officials, and contribute illegally to U.S. politicians' campaigns. In reporting on these and other corporate crimes, the press may have occasionally magnified the offenses, but mostly it has simply mirrored governmental actions and public concerns.

Labor and the Media

Business is far from alone in feeling victimized by the news media. Labor doesn't like its press coverage either. The AFL–CIO complains that the news media slight the 98 percent of collective bargaining that ends in peaceful settlements, while often sensationalizing the 2 percent that results in work stoppages. As a consequence, "most people who read newspapers would never know that the amount of time lost to strikes is less than time lost to the common cold," according to Albert J. Zack, AFL–CIO public relations director.

Union officials complain that stories on contract negotiations typically refer to company "offers," implying generosity, while calling union requests "demands." They say strike stories play up disruption and hardship to the public, while ignoring the hardships that impel workers to go on strike. Strike stories also play up lost sales to local merchants, while slighting the benefits to these same merchants and other businesses from wage settlements that put more disposable income in workers' pockets. But what rankles many union leaders most is that the media devote considerably more attention to corporate suites than to factory floors, to executives than to workers, to affluent suburbs than to working-class neighborhoods. The *Chicago Tribune* used to have a twice-weekly "Blue Collar Views" column, but Mike LaVelle, the common laborer who wrote the column, gave it up in 1978. And few, if any, other dailies have anything similar.

Corporate Misdeeds

Businessmen who have visions of platoons of Woodwards and Bernsteins sneaking around digging up dirt to "get" them underestimate the effectiveness of corporate security and secretiveness. As Columbia University sociologist Herbert Gans observes in *Deciding What's News*: "Journalists readily run news about business corruption when it becomes available, much as they do about political corruption, but private firms have been fairly successful in blocking access to investigative reporters out to expose business misdeeds."

Even misdeeds that involve questionable business activities rather than out-and-out crimes are difficult to uncover. Corporations with something to hide usually are uncooperative with reporters, and the complexity of the issues involved and the need for precision to avoid libel suits make such investigations particularly demanding. Understandably, most business reporters prefer to concentrate on easier-to-cover stories that reflect favorably or neutrally on business.

Possibly because of this, the toughest and most extensive reporting on corporate malfeasance is to be found not in newspapers and magazines, not on television and radio, but in books. Starting in the early 1960s with Rachel Carson's *Silent Spring* on pesticide dangers, Jessica Mitford's *The American Way of Death* on funeral frauds, and Ralph Nader's *Unsafe at Any Speed* on automobile hazards, scores of authors, many of them nonjournalists, have created a wave of muckraking that already dwarfs in scope and duration the golden age of muckraking of 1902-12.

Business seems to have learned to live with the outpouring of books slamming nuclear power, corporate corruption, and industrial damage to the environment, perhaps because a successful book may reach only 20,000 buyers, whereas 12 million American households watch the "CBS Evening News."

Though businessmen angry at the media seldom note it, the most striking aspect of TV coverage of business is how little there is of it. The networks have so little time—22 minutes after commercials and announcements—to report the most important news of the day that all but the most significant and interesting business news gets left out. Business stories most likely to make the air focus on White House announcements, congressional hearings, and other developments laden with audience-pleasing conflict and confrontation. Such stories tend to put business in a bad light even when business's rebuttal is included, as it usually is.

Like network news, newspaper front pages tend to contain more negative stories (corporate overcharges, faulty products, monopolistic practices) than positive stories (corporations creating jobs, cooperating with the community, making technological innovations). But business and financial sections have the opposite orientation. Replete with corporate profit reports, executive promotion announcements, and other stories initiated by corporations, newspaper business sections generally more than offset the negative cast of page one.

Researchers at the University of Minnesota who studied business coverage in four Minneapolis and St. Paul newspapers over a four-month period in 1978-79 found that 56 percent of the stories were neutral, 25 percent reflected favorably on business, and only 19 percent were unfavorable. "If the Twin Cities dailies lean at all, they lean toward business," the researchers concluded. A similar study at the University of North Carolina found 54 percent of stories about business in the *Raleigh News & Observer* neutral, while 20 percent reflected favorably on business and 26 percent unfavorably. "In general, unfavorable impressions of business seemed to be linked to unfavorable news and not to media misrepresentation," the researchers concluded.

Some studies show a correlation between business news and the national economy. Favorable news about business fell during the energy shortage and recession of 1973-75, rose during the economic upturn of 1976-78, then fell again in 1979 as the economy weakened, fuel prices soared, and the nuclear accident at Three Mile Island raised doubts about corporate competence and the future of nuclear power.

**Increased
Business
Reporting**

As resource depletion, inflation, unemployment, and other economic problems have pushed business news onto page one, many newspapers have beefed up their business reporting staffs and started to cover business as closely as they long have covered city hall and the board of education. This has forced business leaders into uncomfortable visibility and unaccustomed accountability, and sometimes strained their relations with the local media.

Des Moines provides a case study. In 1975 the *Des Moines Register* had a business news staff of two. By 1980 there were 10. Among other projects, the enlarged staff kept busy compiling periodic surveys of the salaries of hundreds of top executives of Iowa corporations. Businessmen complained that these "How Much Does Your Boss Make?" surveys invaded their privacy, complicated wage negotiations with unions, and could even encourage criminals to rob their homes and kidnap their children. Similar objections were raised to publication of lists of Des Moines homes with the highest tax assessments.

Editor Michael Gartner defended such coverage as in keeping with the Fourth Estate's function of gathering and distributing matters of public record that "are available to anyone, but that would be difficult and time-consuming for each person to dig out." As for criminals reading the paper to determine who the wealthy are, "anyone driving around Des Moines can tell where the rich live, congregate, work, and play."

Other complaints against the *Des Moines Register* included charges that coverage of a long and bitter labor dispute was sympathetic to the strikers. Many businessmen thought an investigative

story of two Boston promoters who used a Des
Moines bank to "launder" part of $20 million
received from investors in a coal mine tax shelter
unfairly implied the bank knew the money was
tainted. And friends of Des Moines' leading banker
were outraged at a brief item that the banker was
undergoing treatment for alcoholism.

The story on the alcoholic banker rankled so
deeply that editor Gartner felt compelled to offer
readers an explanation: "We printed the story because John (Fitzgibbon) is a big man around town.
When he got the job, it was news. When he led the
bank to growth and continued success, it was news.
And when he went on medical leave, it was news—
probably bigger news than we made it."

Such explanations failed to mollify many Des
Moines businessmen. William Friedman, Jr., president of Younkers department store, which at one
point stopped advertising in the *Register* because
"we felt they had been picking on us," complained
that in general the paper puts "too much emphasis
on what's wrong and not enough on what's right
about business and the free enterprise system.
There's a definite liberal bias in the reporting." J. B.
Walters, manager of the local Firestone Tire and
Rubber Company plant, went further. "Socialistic
in nature and detrimental to the survival of the private enterprise system" was his view of the *Register*'s coverage and commentary.

Be that as it may, when Walters and other businessmen making general charges against the *Register* were asked to cite specific stories they considered slanted, close examination of these stories
usually revealed the complaints to be trivial or unjustified. For instance, a six-part series on work-

place health hazards that Firestone's Walters called "inflammatory" turned out to be a well-documented, calm, and balanced presentation of a significant issue. Far from leaving the impression that Firestone "totally destroyed" the health of one of its Des Moines employees, as Walters contended, the series pointed out that the Firestone employee was awarded only 20 percent disability benefits, and it extensively reported company assurances that any workplace hazards had been corrected.

James P. Gannon, the *Register's* executive editor, traced much of the Des Moines business community's animosity to its faulty perception of the journalist's role. "A businessman judges a story by its effects—good or bad—on his business, and assumes that if the effect is harmful to his business, the reporter who wrote it must have intended to do damage. But reporters and editors judge a story not by its effect on a business but on whether it is interesting and significant."

Many businessmen don't see it that way, of course. The folks at McDonnell Douglas Corporation, for instance, thought that the news media overplayed the American Airlines DC-10 crash that took 275 lives in Chicago in 1979, and that some segments of the press gave the company and the airplane an unjustified "pillorying." McDonnell Douglas was particularly aggrieved at some newspaper cartoons. These included a Pat Oliphant cartoon in the *Washington Star* showing a DC-10 engine and engine mount falling apart at a single hammer blow, a Bill Schorr cartoon in the *Los Angeles Herald Examiner* likening the DC-10 to the Edsel automobile, and a Lee Judge cartoon in the *San Diego Union* suggesting that the DC-10 was a "lemon."

Then there were three cartoons that Paul Conrad drew for the *Los Angeles Times*. The first showed a Volkswagen Beetle parked next to a DC–10, and posed the question, "Which of these vehicles has more bolts holding its engine on?" The second cartoon, which prompted 53 critical letters to the *Times* and none in support, showed DC–10 passengers in flight being startled by the announcement, "This is the president of McDonnell Douglas speaking . . . welcome aboard the *Titanic*. . . ." The third cartoon, appearing several months later, showed a McDonnell Douglas DC–9 in flight losing its tail cone (as an Air Canada DC–9 had just done).

"THIS IS THE PRESIDENT OF McDONNELL DOUGLAS SPEAKING.... WELCOME ABOARD THE TITANIC...."

Source: © 1979, *Los Angeles Times.* Reprinted with permission.

"We're OK—It's not an engine," the pilot announced reassuringly.

Funny as the DC–9 and DC–10 cartoons were to many people, they struck McDonnell Douglas as cruel and crude. Some news stories also displeased the company. One, by the Associated Press, reported that despite the Chicago DC–10 crash and the DC–9 tail cone incident, two airlines were placing orders for the "problem-plagued" planes. A company spokesman complained that the phrase *problem-plagued* unfairly cast an otherwise positive story in a negative light. But he seemed oversensitive. Both planes were indeed plagued by problems, not all of which the AP even mentioned. Nor did AP remind readers that Italy's national airline, Alitalia, had previously cancelled an order for the DC–10s, deciding to buy Boeing Company's 747 jets instead.

All stories and cartoons considered, the press didn't pillory McDonnell Douglas. Of course, in the Soviet Union a similar plane crash probably would not have been reported at all. Soviet authorities don't like to admit openly that anything has gone wrong, so disasters are rarely covered. If, in contrast, the U.S. news media seem obsessed with disasters, it is not solely a matter of pandering to the public's unwholesome morbidity, but also a method for pressuring government authorities to take corrective action.

As both the DC–10 and Des Moines flaps make clear, the time has come for businessmen once accustomed to uncritical and even promotional coverage to resign themselves to receiving the same kind of probing and even impolite press that politicians have had to endure for decades. With the bus-

iness of America more than ever business, it seems
reasonable to hold the people who run industry
and commerce as accountable as the people who
run government.

However, journalists need to be sure that skepti-
cism about business does not sour into cynicism.
A business executive who becomes a public figure
may waive his right to privacy, as the *Des Moines
Register* contends, but a newspaper's reputation
for fairness is an even more precious asset than its
reputation for completeness. Avoiding even the
appearance of nastiness poses an extra considera-
tion in publishing stories such as the one on the
banker undergoing treatment for alcoholism.

All coverage considered, there is no question that
bad news about business has been on the rise. But
business attempts to blame the bad-news boom for
turning public opinion against it mostly ring hol-
low. Any American who has waited in line to buy
gasoline, had a flight reservation "lost" in a computer, phoned in an order only to be put on hold, or
put in time for an impersonal conglomerate, already has strong views about business. To business,
that's the worst news of all.

2

Newspapers: Muddled, Not Malicious

When the General Accounting Office reported on its investigation into whether American oil producers had deliberately worsened the 1979 oil shortage, it was a case of which newspaper do you read:

G.A.O. STUDY ASSERTS
THAT OIL COMPANIES
WORSENED SHORTAGE
New York Times

GAO Says Oil Firms
Aren't to Be Blamed
For Recent Shortage
Wall Street Journal

According to the *New York Times* story, the General Accounting Office, which is the investigatory arm of Congress, found that "American oil companies had aggravated last spring's petroleum shortage by cutting production of crude oil within the United States last winter while imports from Iran were disrupted." But according to *The Wall Street Journal* story, which ran the same day, the GAO concluded "there isn't any evidence that the major oil companies created the U.S. oil shortage that occurred after the closing of Iran's oil fields."

21

As it turned out, *The Wall Street Journal* was right and the *New York Times* was wrong. Acknowledging as much, the *Times* ran a lengthy correction two days later, saying it had misinterpreted the GAO's report. Other newspapers had still other versions. The *Los Angeles Times,* for instance, didn't even mention the GAO's judgment on oil company culpability, focusing instead on GAO criticism of Department of Energy actions.

If three of the nation's biggest and best newspapers couldn't agree on the contents of a government document, it is hardly surprising that smaller and less well-staffed dailies also get things mixed up. Indeed, the nation's 1,750 daily newspapers are far more often guilty of muddled coverage of business news than of malicious coverage. Simplistic treatment is far more prevalent than sensationalism. One-sided stories are common, but usually they contain only business's side, not its critics'. And antibusiness bias isn't nearly as noticeable as uncritical acceptance of business positions.

Indeed, the evidence that newspapers flail businessmen seems a lot less persuasive than that newspapers fail readers by not relating business news to the concerns of the man in the street. The steady diet of colorless, cut-and-dried business stories and stock and bond statistics that newspapers serve up may fascinate businessmen and investors, but surveys show they prompt most readers to flip the page.

Efforts to Improve Coverage

Less relevant and readable than it might be, newspaper business coverage is at least better than it used to be. Even businessmen attest to that. Citicorp Chairman Walter B. Wriston, who previously had accused the media of "sniping" at business, said in 1979 that "the papers I read are substantially better than they were 10 years ago." Herbert Schmertz, Mobil Corporation's outspoken vice president–public affairs, judged that television did a worse job of covering the 1979 energy shortage and price runup than it had the 1973–74 energy crunch. But he concluded that newspaper coverage had "very significantly improved," becoming "more balanced, realistic, intelligent, and informed."

The upsurge of energy and other business and economic news in the early 1970s caught the press as unprepared as the civil rights movement had a decade earlier. In the early 1960s, newspapers suddenly needed reporters who could hit the streets and get the story from demonstrators. The business news boom 10 years later put newspapers in need of reporters who could walk into corporate offices and get the story from executives.

Despite a shortage of experienced business reporters, most metropolitan dailies have beefed up their business news staffs and are devoting more space to business news. A number of metros have even liberated business news from the rear of the sports section to which it traditionally has been consigned, awarding it a separate section. The *New York Times* was the first, in 1978, to publish a separate business section every weekday, followed two years later by the *Los Angeles Times.* Other papers that introduced separate business sections on one or more weekdays included the *Chicago Tribune, Boston Globe,* and *Washington Post.*

However, the increase in business news hasn't always been matched by a comparable increase in

staff, so that even metropolitan dailies often give
reporters too little time to research complex sub-
jects and write in-depth reports. Short staffing is
endemic at smaller papers. A 1977 survey found
that the 93 percent of American dailies with less
than 100,000 circulation typically had a business
news staff of only one, and even medium-sized
papers of 100,000 to 250,000 had only four. At
most dailies, business editors are pressed just to
answer the phone, process routine news releases,
edit wire service copy and make up the business
page. Reporters often have little time for face-to-
face interviews, relying on the phone instead.

Although business coverage appeals to an increasing number of reporters, many find it dull and
boring and they jump at any opportunity to trans-
fer to livelier beats, forcing editors to break in
replacements and local businesses to put up with
naive novices.

Inexperienced reporters turned loose on complex stories they cannot help but mangle do considerably more harm to business than do biased
reporters who deliberately set out to "get" business, both journalists and businessmen agree.
Donald Kirsch, a New York financial public relations executive, said: "My clients aren't afraid of
their warts being revealed, but they are afraid of
reporters making mistakes and misinterpreting
their actions and decisions."

Recognizing that naive and muddled coverage
isn't in business's interest, a number of major corporations and foundations now underwrite university programs aimed at upgrading business reporters' skills. Columbia, Carnegie-Mellon, Missouri,
and several other universities have fellowship pro-

grams to give reporters intensive instruction in business and economics and then return them to their newspapers. Chris Welles, director of the Walter Bagehot Fellowship Program at Columbia, said: "These programs may not make reporters probusiness, but they do make them more knowledgeable and less likely to go off on ill-informed attacks."

Criticisms of Coverage

Of course, even knowledgeable journalists are sometimes misinformed. The usually astute editors of *Automotive News,* a respected weekly newspaper for the automobile industry, thought they had a major scoop in 1979 when sources told them that Volkswagen, the West German auto giant, was negotiating to acquire ailing Chrysler Corporation. Although both companies denied the story, *Automotive News* broke it and the general-interest press picked it up. The deal never happened, however, and *Automotive News* refused to disclose where it got its information, which it continued to defend.

Although the Volkswagen-Chrysler story seems to have done little if any harm, businessmen complain that many errors cause unnecessary damage because they aren't corrected promptly and prominently enough. Instead of correcting a front-page error inside the paper, which is standard practice, newspapers ought to correct it on the front page under a headline as large as the original, the argument goes. Whatever added embarrassment the front-page correction would cause might be more than offset by enhanced credibility and reader goodwill.

Another complaint against newspapers is their propensity to print incomplete stories. Many of these are caused by daily deadlines that cut off reporting on a story before important facts and proper perspective are obtained. An incomplete story on, say, a Federal Trade Commission action can make business look worse than it would otherwise. "I have no sympathy for deadline problems," Mobil's Schmertz said, because they are caused by competitive business considerations, not journalistic necessity. "If a story is incomplete, it ought to be held for a day. It's better to report it a day late, but fully."

Still another charge against newspapers is sensationalism. Sensationalism was common a generation or two ago when most cities of any size had several separately owned dailies competing on newsstands for reader attention. But today most newspapers have no direct competition and are mostly home-delivered. They no longer need sensationalism to sell copies. Yet sensationalism hasn't died out completely, lingering in some of the few remaining competitive markets.

The *Washington Post* was charged with sensationalism in 1976 when it front-paged a story that revealed the U.S. Comptroller of the Currency had placed two of the nation's largest banks, First National City (now Citibank) and Chase Manhattan, on a confidential list of "problem" banks that had made many risky loans and required extra-close federal supervision. Although the story was legitimate, splashing it across the top of page one over-emphasized the severity of the banks' problems and left the *Washington Post* vulnerable to charges of sensationalism.

The New York *Daily News,* largest of a dwindling breed of tabloids, has often riled businessmen with headlines that exaggerate. For instance, the *News*'s headline on a 1979 story about a Federal Trade Commission study critical of life insurance was "FTC: SOME LIFE POLICIES ARE RIP-OFFS," even though the FTC hadn't used the word "rip-off." "That's a very tough word to compete against," complained Robert A. Beck, chairman of Prudential Insurance Company of America.

And even the most sober papers exaggerate the ups and downs of the stock market. To the *Los Angeles Times*, "STOCKS SOAR" when the Dow Jones industrial average gains nine points, or a mere 1 percent, and the "DOW TUMBLES" when the index loses 15 points, or less than 2 percent. Playing up day-to-day fluctuations in stock prices obscures the reality that prices tend to even out over time and that the Dow Jones industrial average has been flat for several years. And treating the misnamed Dow Jones industrial average (it's actually an index, not an average) as though it were a reliable barometer of the stock market ignores the fact that it measures the price movements of only 30 blue-chip stocks out of 1,500 common stocks listed on the New York Stock Exchange, and that during the 1970s it considerably underestimated the average price rise of Big Board stocks.

Business initiates most business news through news releases that newspapers typically process with only minor alterations. And many of the stories that newspapers initiate are glowing profiles of successful entrepreneurs, optimistic forecasts of corporate expansion, and heartwarming accounts of community-spirited business projects.

Reporters specializing in business coverage generally are more sympathetic to business than generalists, who are more likely to quote populist politicians, public-interest advocates, and other business critics. However, even more sympathetic than business reporters are editorial writers who assume that businessmen have the public interest at heart and are working to build a better America.

Business expansion is good for the local economy, of course, and what's good for the local economy is good for the local newspaper. For this reason, among others, newspapers generally endorse development projects even when environmental and health hazards are associated with them. For instance, the Pasco (Wash.) *Tri-City Herald* promotes commercial dumping of radioactive nuclear wastes at the government's nearby Hanford Nuclear Reservation. Its stories have carried such headlines as "WASTE COULD BE $20-BILLION HANFORD BUSINESS" and "HARRISBURG ACCIDENT COULD BENEFIT HANFORD."

Newspapers rarely question the basic orientation of the local economy. Exceptions are as rare as they are noteworthy. In 1979 the *Charlotte Observer* published a 20-page news supplement devoted to a hard look at the tobacco industry, on which North Carolina's economy is heavily dependent. The supplement assessed the industry's economic and political influence. It reviewed the medical evidence that cigarette smoking is hazardous and advised readers how to break the smoking habit. And it editorialized both that the tobacco industry should stop denying the dangers of smoking and that the federal government should start labeling cigarettes as "addictive."

Although the *Observer* stopped short of suggesting stronger measures such as higher cigarette taxes, segregation of smokers from nonsmokers in public places, and an end to federal price supports for tobacco, its supplement was considered daring in a state whose farmers count on tobacco as their No. 1 cash crop and whose factories turn out nearly 1 billion cigarettes a day. "It took courage," said managing editor Mark Ethridge III. Yet no cigarette manufacturer pulled its advertising or even complained openly, indicating that even in an industry-dependent economy newspapers can practice a lot tougher journalism than most do. Indeed, a good case can be made that in the vast majority of American cities, including Charlotte, without competing newspapers under separate ownership, advertisers and businessmen need the local paper at least as much as the local paper needs them.

Be that as it may, local newspapers continue to give business editorial support on national as well as local issues. For instance, 85 percent of the newspapers that took a position on the issue of whether the Federal Trade Commission should restrict television advertising to children opposed such restrictions. And 98 percent of the papers taking a position on congressional moves to break up the giant oil companies opposed vertical divestiture. Such overwhelming endorsement of Big Oil's position hasn't been left to chance. Boasted the American Petroleum Institute: "There probably isn't a major daily newspaper in the country that has not been visited by oil company spokesmen—many of them at top executive levels—for an editorial board discussion laying out industry views on divestiture."

Even when businessmen strike out with editorial writers, they can usually still manage to get their views across to newspaper readers. John J. Nevin, chairman of Zenith Radio Corporation, couldn't

persuade the *New York Times* to come out for
stricter enforcement of laws prohibiting the dumping of underpriced foreign television sets and other
goods in the United States, but he did get the
Times in 1979 to publish two guest columns in
which he set forth his case.

Businessmen sometimes manage to woo both
editorial writers and reporters. Breakfast cereal
manufacturers fighting a Federal Trade Commission antitrust suit seeking to break them up won
New York Times support not only in an editorial
but also in a business section article that repeated
defendant Kellogg Company's objections to the
"un-American" antitrust suit without including
any rebuttal from the FTC.

Although such one-sided coverage generally is in
business's favor, there are instances in which it
works the other way. When the FTC issued its
1979 report critical of life insurance, the New York
Daily News failed to include industry reaction in
its story. Nor did the *News* cover the industry's
rebuttal testimony before a Senate committee
several months later. *The Wall Street Journal* also
ignored the rebuttal testimony, even though it had
covered the original report. The issue of whether
whole-life insurance is a good buy is as much a consumer story as a business story. Yet with the notable exception of the *Hartford Courant,* few papers
bothered to cut through the claims and complexities and clarify the issue to help readers make up
their own mind on what kind of life insurance, if
any, to buy.

Rather than broaden and deepen their business
coverage to interest general readers, most news-

papers continue to wrap bland news releases from local businesses and wire service stories from New York and Washington around column after column of stock and bond tables, commodity futures prices, foreign exchange rates, and other minutiae of interest to only a small fraction of their readers. Many newspapers actually are publishing additional stock tables despite evidence that the public is turning its back on stocks, which proved such a poor investment in the 1970s that returns to investors in price appreciation and dividends trailed inflation. The New York Stock Exchange has estimated that the number of individual Americans owning stock dropped by 1 million between 1970 and 1980, leaving stocks more than ever the province of banks, pension funds and other institutional investors.

According to a 1978 Big Board survey, only 13 percent of the nation's affluent households have a brokerage account and a mere 2 percent actively trade stocks. Yet newspaper editors assume that even inactive investors like to check the market price of stocks they own, once owned, or would like to own, and that the stock tables are as important to them as baseball box scores, comic strips, and the horoscope column are to their fans. The difference is that the stock tables take up much more space and aren't consulted daily by most who follow them.

Cutting back on stock tables and other financial esoterica would free a lot of space that could be used for in-depth articles of interest to general readers as well as investors. The audience is there. According to a University of North Carolina School of Journalism survey, the public is more interested in coverage of national and local business, new products, and how business works than it is in the stock market.

Of course, stock tables are cheap copy requiring minimum handling, whereas covering national and local business, new products, and how business works requires reporters. Fortunately, newspapers can afford a lot more reporters. Profit margins are typically high and news budgets relatively low, averaging 9 percent of all operating expenses for large dailies. Many newspapers could double their news budgets and still reap higher profit margins than most industries enjoy.

In the end, then, the failure of American newspapers is not that they are too hard on business but that they are too easy on themselves. Secure in their markets, most daily newspapers still starve their business pages on a diet of inadequate space and staff, and settle for dull, fragmented, cursory coverage when what is increasingly needed is critical analysis of complex business issues of interest and relevance to all readers.

3

Clamming Up
Doesn't Pay

Bank of America and its vice chairman, Alvin C.
Rice, parted company in 1978 in a dispute over
Rice's private investments with a customer of the
bank. The investments were an apparent violation
of bank policy and Rice was asked to leave. The
54-year-old Rice had been considered the heir
apparent to the presidency of the bank and its
parent, BankAmerica Corporation, but did the
world have to be told why he left? No. Despite a
months-old "model" disclosure code intended to
make the bank more open with the news media
and the public, the bank sent out a three-sentence
news release saying only that Rice was resigning
"to pursue personal business opportunities." It
stonewalled reporters seeking further information,
saying Rice's right to privacy superseded the public's right to know.

The real story came out only months later, after
Bank of America had issued a second uninformative and misleading news release. By then, the bank
had alienated reporters, and its attempted coverup
had backfired into what *Business Week* called "the
banking industry's biggest public relations blunder
in years."

Far from being an isolated case, the Rice affair demonstrates how business often contributes to its problems with the press and its credibility gap with the public. From the largest and best managed corporations to the smallest and least professional, businesses frequently duck reporters, cover up problems, issue deceptive information, and invite the increasingly critical coverage they deplore.

It is true that many corporations have opened up in recent years. For more than a century, Adolph Coors Company operated on the premise that it needed only to brew good beer. But a bitter two-year labor dispute and union-organized boycott tarnished its image and cost it customers, leading it to the reluctant conclusion it could no longer hide behind its proud label. So instead of paying public relations people to keep Coors's name out of the papers, the company took to drumming up coverage with ads explaining its new openness and inviting reporters to "call us toll free."

Some industries also are entering the 20th century of corporate accountability and professional public relations. The oil industry, which used to treat the news media with indifference and even disdain, was forced by the oil shortage and price runup of 1973-74 to defend itself against charges it contrived the shortage and reaped inordinate profits from it. Since then, most big oil companies have expanded their public relations staffs, made executives more available for interviews, and shown greater willingness to discuss their operations. Not every oil company is equally responsive, of course. Mobil Corporation generally refuses television interviews that are subject to network editing, and 't is combative about coverage it doesn't like. And even when its annual sales topped $6 billion, Amerada Hess Corporation was still functioning without a public relations department and failing to return reporters' calls.

A Suspicious Silence

The airline, computer, and banking industries generally rate high among journalists for openness. The food, tobacco, pharmaceutical, and retailing industries are considered tight-lipped. "The healthier economically and more honest morally an industry is, the more open it is," according to ABC correspondent David Marash. "Industries clam up when they have something to hide. The defense industry doesn't want to talk about inefficiency. The construction industry doesn't want to talk about labor-management relations."

Then too, a surprising number of very large corporations are still run as one-man shows by ruggedly independent entrepreneurs who like to do things their way. Take Harcourt Brace Jovanovich Inc. and its long-time chief executive, William Jovanovich. The company, which publishes books and periodicals and operates Sea World amusement parks, has no corporate public relations staff because Chairman Jovanovich likes to handle corporate PR himself. But when he is unavailable or unwilling to be interviewed, reporters are out of luck.

When the company folded *Human Nature* in 1979, Jovanovich instructed the magazine's staff to give out no interviews or details. "It is idle to indulge in speculation on past events," he explained in a memo. *Folio*, a trade journal for the magazine industry, sought further information but was rebuffed, whereupon it scored Harcourt Brace

Jovanovich's "turn-of-the-century approach to public relations" as particularly inappropriate for the publisher of some 30 trade journals. Jovanovich dismissed *Folio*'s complaint as improper, saying he didn't want to discuss the death of *Human Nature* for internal reasons and because "we hadn't learned what the hell the problem was." Besides, he added, "the First Amendment doesn't give the press the right to have every telephone call and every question answered."

Like Jovanovich, many chief executives seem to resent any outsider passing judgment on a company to which they have devoted much of their adult lives. Some seem frustrated that they can't buy media coverage the way they purchase supplies and services. A few want things printed the company way or not at all. When a *Los Angeles Times* reporter phoned an oil company president to clarify a news release on a new gasoline pricing policy, he was told, "Just run it the way I sent it in, sonny."

Such arrogance is not unusual. "There are still quite a few executive officers who are accustomed to giving orders and who resent the media for not taking them," Kenneth A. Randall, president of the Conference Board, the business research group, said. Michael Gartner, editor of the *Des Moines Register* and the *Des Moines Tribune,* has noticed the same thing. "Chief executives eventually reach the point where their word is law—in their company, in their family, in the industry organizations they belong to. No one ever tells them they are wrong, or even things they don't want to hear. The only aspects of their lives that they can't control are the government and the press. It's useless to fight the government, but the press is up front and they can fight it."

At most large corporations, chief executives delegate fighting and other contact with the news media to well-staffed public relations departments. At Procter & Gamble Company in Cincinnati, PR staffers answer routine inquiries, provide background information, and shield executives from unwanted media attention by discouraging reporters from contacting them. Reporters half-joke that arranging an audience with the Pope is easier than getting an interview with the president of P&G.

At some companies, public relations staffers are as much a hindrance as a help to reporters. For instance, a Zenith Radio Corporation PR executive promised a *Los Angeles Times* reporter he would set up an interview with Zenith's chief executive but then didn't follow through. When contacted directly, the chief executive talked freely for an hour and a half. At other corporations, the runaround is routine. General Foods Corporation's public relations department took five weeks to mail public relations materials it had promised one reporter, and then only after he had contacted the company's chief executive directly and explained his project.

News Manipulation by Business

To be fair, companies sometimes delay responses because they haven't had time to study the government action or other development they're asked to comment on. And some companies are speeding up responses in the realization that it improves their chances of getting favorable stories. But many balk as much as ever.

Some PR people tell reporters as little as possible to avoid saying something indiscreet that will be reported and get them in trouble with their superiors. Others seem to hope that reporters with embarrassing questions will get discouraged and drop their stories. "Too often, corporate PR people operate under the assumption that if they say nothing, we won't broadcast anything, or if we do they will be able to claim we weren't fair," Av Westin, an ABC News vice president, said.

Reversing journalists' usual news judgment, PR people routinely accentuate the positive and de-emphasize the negative. Itel Corporation, the deficit-beset computer leasing concern, led a 1979 news release with the good news that it "had received waivers of certain financial covenants from its banks and institutional lenders," and subordinated the bad news that Itel's losses would be substantially greater than earlier forecast.

Even when bad news can't be buried, it can be released at inconvenient times; for instance, just before deadline—so that reporters have little or no time to get elaboration. Another ploy is to release the bad news on Friday in the knowledge that readership of Saturday newspapers is lower than on weekdays. Better still, think some companies, don't release the bad news at all. When McDonald's Corporation cut the price of its regular hamburgers five cents in 1979, it proclaimed the move in news releases and TV commercials. But three months later, when it hiked prices of its big hamburgers, fried potatoes and soft drinks by as much as 11 cents, the fast food chain didn't even put out a news release.

Candor is especially vulnerable at times of embarrassing executive departures, such as vice chairman Rice's from Bank of America. In 1979, Walt Disney Productions Inc. made no announcement when eight animators and three directors of animation quit over creative differences to form their own production studio.

Corporations in the news media business seem as reluctant as most to air their dirty linen in public. When Washington Post Company forced out President Larry H. Israel in 1977 and *Newsweek* Editor Edward Kosner in 1979, its press releases were so uninformative that reporters seeking reasons for the resignations had to tap other sources. And the *New York Times,* although it regularly reports price increases in many industries, refused in 1979 to specify increases in its own advertising rates to its own advertising columnist.

Sometimes circumstances justify reticence. Corporation lawyers may advise against making any public statement that could be used against a company in a future legal action. Or news that could affect a company's stock price may be withheld from one reporter because of fear of Securities and Exchange Commission displeasure that the news wasn't released simultaneously to all investors. More often, however, the SEC provides just a convenient excuse.

Fear of demoralizing employees and upsetting their unions occasionally prompts companies to clam up. "If we had anything positive to say, we would say it," an official of Firestone Tire and Rubber Company told a reporter inquiring about rumors that Firestone would lay off workers at its Los Angeles tire plant and eventually close it down.

The Trouble with Stonewalling

However, "no comment" can cause more harm to a company's image than good. As James P. Gannon, executive editor of the *Des Moines Regis-*

ter, observed: "It didn't help Ford Motor Company to deny that it knew of any problem with its Pinto automobile, and it didn't help Firestone Tire to stonewall the press about the problems with its radial 500 tire. Those stories came out anyway and the companies only worsened the situation." Indeed, difficulty in getting information tends to confirm a reporter's suspicions that a company has something to hide, and may reinforce his determination to get the story by some other means. This can lead to a more critical story, and even an inaccurate one.

Business Week, which used to drop a story if the company involved declined cooperation, nowadays goes ahead with such stories even at the risk of missing and messing up facts. When Westinghouse Electric Corporation refused to grant interviews for a cover story contrasting Westinghouse's problems with competitor General Electric Company's progress, on the grounds that it "had said everything that needed to be said," the magazine nonetheless pieced together the story. However, *Business Week* peppered the story with quotations from Westinghouse executives that it had gathered nearly two years earlier for a story it never ran, without alerting readers that the remarks were dated. And it made a lot of errors—31 by the company's count. Westinghouse Chairman Robert E. Kirby, whose name the article got wrong, shot off a letter blasting the piece as "unbalanced and blemished with inaccuracies." But the errors weren't corrected nor the damage to Westinghouse's reputation soon undone.

Speak No Evil— Or Else

Some companies have been known to penalize news organizations that displease them by cutting off all communication with them for years. General Dynamics Corporation's Electric Boat division in Groton, Conn., clamped a news blackout against the *New London Day* in 1978 after the newspaper reported production errors, delays, and cost overruns on the nuclear-powered submarines that Electric Boat builds for the Navy. Under the blackout, which lasted three years, Electric Boat refused to send the *Day* news releases or return its reporters' calls. Also, it no longer advertised in the paper. The blackout hurt Electric Boat by making it impossible for the newspaper to do feature stories on engineering accomplishments and other developments that would have reflected credit on management. But management seemed less interested in restoring relations than in retribution. When the National News Council offered to mediate the dispute, Electric Boat refused even to talk to the media-monitoring group's staff.

Some companies have carried retaliation even further. Take Pacific Gas & Electric Company and its attempt to discredit "Powers That Be," a 1971 documentary on the dangers of nuclear energy that Donald Widener produced for Los Angeles television station KNBC. After "Powers That Be" was aired, the company and one of its engineers circulated a letter accusing Widener of secretly taping a pre-interview conversation with the engineer and then splicing portions of that conversation into the documentary, distorting the engineer's remarks. Widener sued for libel, and during the trial the utility admitted its charges were false. After seven years of litigation, Widener settled for $475,000, which he called little enough compensation for the damage to his career.

The nuclear industry's acute sensitivity is far from uncommon. David Finn of the New York public relations firm of Ruder and Finn thinks that "businessmen often overreact to press criticism. Living in fear of press exposure can lead to a sort of paranoia. One has to learn to take criticism in stride."

A Spirit of Cooperation

Fortunately for the future of business-press relations, an increasing number of business executives are learning to take criticism in stride. One such is James L. Ferguson, chairman of General Foods Corporation. In 1976, Ferguson told a group of advertising executives that "at General Foods, we have been angry at the press, or outraged or shocked or disappointed or perplexed a number of times in the past few years." Among the grievances: alarmist coverage of product safety, "sloppiness," "underlying hostility," and even "flagrant bias."

Four years later, General Foods still had complaints, but Ferguson credited the news media for "an increasing level of competence and sophistication" in reporting business news. Press hostility toward business is "less in evidence, or I react to it less," he said, and both sides have a better understanding of the other's point of view. "The press isn't as aggressive, as shrill, as uncompromising as it used to be, and I'm not as defensive."

Some corporate executives have gone beyond dropping defensiveness to kissing and making up with the media. Westinghouse Chairman Kirby forgave *Business Week* for its negative story and two years later allowed the magazine to use his name, photograph, and remarks in a house ad promoting corporate-issue advertising.

As Kirby remarked in the *Business Week* ad, expansion-minded businesses face increasing risks from "construction stoppages, potential product bans, vaguely written laws," and "drastic regulation." He added: "We recognize that silence can turn issues into risks, so our goal is to be known as a communicating company."

To communicate with the American public, companies must first communicate with the media. And as more and more businessmen are discovering, the price of good communication with the media is cooperation and candor.

4

Television: Snappy and Superficial

At the height of 1979's gasoline lines, the president of Mobil Corporation went to Washington to testify before a congressional committee about his company's maverick oil proposals. William P. Tavoulareas had spent several hours quietly explaining Mobil's position on price controls (retain them on already discovered oil, remove them on yet-to-be-discovered oil) and the proposed windfall-profits tax (no), when a Democratic congressman from New Jersey confronted him.

Holding up a poster marked "No Decontrol" for the benefit of the ABC News television cameras covering the hearing, Representative Andrew Maguire declared he had received 13,000 such messages from angry constituents. He then proceeded to flail Mobil and other oil producers for price-gouging, profiteering, and deserving the public's distrust. Tavoulareas defended Mobil for a few minutes, then lost patience and stalked out of the hearing room with his aides, leaving the congressman declaiming to an empty witness table.

In reporting on the hearing that evening, ABC's "World News Tonight" focused on the confrontation between the combative oil man and the grand-standing congressman, all but ignoring the substance of Mobil's testimony. Spotlighting the entertaining clash rather than the dull testimony was standard TV practice, but to Mobil it was a deplorable example of how television news overplays conflict, oversimplifies issues, encourages irresponsible behavior by politicians, and shortchanges the public on basic information.

**TV News:
Anti-Big
Business?**

Mobil's low opinion of TV news is shared by other oil producers and by big business in general. While regarding most newspapers and newsmagazines as neutral-to-sympathetic, the oil industry looks on television as often unfriendly, inaccurate, and superficial—and at least partly responsible for turning public opinion against it. Large corporations especially resent TV for biting the hand that feeds it. Television has no income other than what it gets from corporate advertisers, who poured more than $11 billion into TV in 1980. As Leonard S. Matthews, president of the American Association of Advertising Agencies, warned, "To expect private companies to go on supporting a medium that is attacking them is like taking up a collection among Christians for money to buy more lions."

However, what business executives like Matthews consider persecution often is little more than TV doing what it does best. By the nature of the medium, television is better suited to capture high drama and transmit emotional experience than it is to present detailed information and explain complex issues. If TV news served only to supplement fuller accounts in newspapers and news magazines, its concentration on entertaining sidelights such as the Tavoulareas-Maguire hearing room skirmish would cause little comment or controversy, because the public would still be getting its basic information and insights elsewhere.

But polls show that most Americans get most of their news, including business news, from television, and here is where the trouble lies. A half-hour news show, reduced to type, fills only half the front page of a standard-sized daily newspaper, necessitating the omission of many important stories and the compression of those that make the air to the point where comprehension is often sacrificed. "You can't tell the whole story in a minute and a quarter," NBC business correspondent Michael C. Jensen explained. "Not only do you have to leave out nuances, you have to leave out major elements."

Although they share in the prosperity created by TV news's huge audiences, network news executives deplore the public's overreliance on TV news. Av Westin, an ABC vice president, has noted: "The evening news is not the highest form of journalism. It is partly an illustrated headline service and partly a magazine. And, yes, it is part show business, using visual enticement and a star system to attract viewers. Television news can function best when it is regarded by its viewers as an important yet fast adjunct to the newspapers. When I read statistics that show most Americans get most of their news from television, I shudder. I know what we have to leave out."

The twin tyrannies of time and pictures condemn many important but nonvisual business stories to TV oblivion. When the staff of the Federal Trade Commission released results of a two-and-a-half-year investigation of whole-life insur-

ance, concluding it was a poor investment for consumers, only one network, NBC, mentioned the
FTC report, and its 30-second snippet left no time
for the complexities involved, much less insurance
industry rebuttal.

While some business stories are condensed to the
point of incomprehensibility, others are cluttered
with show-and-tell gimmicks designed to compen-
sate for the fact that what a viewer hears registers
less readily than what he sees. Business stories involving figures often use visual props to aid comprehension. For instance, ABC economics editor
Dan Cordtz stood in a bank vault and showed
$55,000 in currency to illustrate what a viewer
would have to spend each and every day for 50
years to match Chrysler Corporation's expected
loss of $1 billion in 1979.

Experienced business journalists such as Cordtz,
who put in 19 years at *The Wall Street Journal* and
Fortune magazine before joining ABC News in
1974, are capable of far more profound business
coverage than they usually manage to get on the
air. But the necessity of competing for air time
with usually livelier domestic and foreign stories
forces business reporters to keep their stories simple and visual.

Businessmen give all three networks credit for
hiring business specialists such as Cordtz and making an effort to lift business coverage above the
level of superficiality characteristic of local TV
news. But the networks also employ investigative
reporters whose coverage strikes businessmen as
often adversarial, even accusatory.

Consider Brian Ross of NBC and his investigation of purported improprieties in the oil industry. Ross's reports, split into five segments, were aired on succeeding evenings one week in 1979 on the "NBC Nightly News." In one segment, Ross accused Exxon Corporation of reducing shipments of low-sulphur fuel oil to a Florida utility in favor of supplying more profitable petroleum products to customers in Europe. Although an Exxon executive patiently rebutted the evidence on which Ross based his charges, the key points of the rebuttal never made the air. This outraged Exxon and prompted it to file a complaint with the National News Council, which found the company's complaint warranted.

Ross similarly ignored inconvenient rebuttal in a segment in which he accused Shell Oil Company of "planning to pull out of the home heating oil business in the Northeast," even at the risk of stranding customers in winter. What a Shell official pointed out, but Ross ignored, was evidence that Shell had notified Northeast customers back in 1975 that it planned to pull out, and that far from cutting off any customers, Shell continued to supply the handful that couldn't find alternate sources of supply. Like Exxon, Shell complained to the National News Council, an independent group that monitors media performance. The council ruled in the company's favor, agreeing "there was nothing sudden about Shell's decision or subsequent actions." In a concurring opinion, two National News Council members labeled the Ross report "strident and accusatory," "biased and at times deceitful," and "irresponsible."

Although the council didn't mention it, Ross also was adversarial. His interviews with Shell and Exxon officials seemed designed less to elicit information than to lure them into making damaging admissions. And when they admitted nothing, he rephrased questions repeatedly as though he were a prosecuting attorney cross-examining a recalcitrant witness.

NBC, which stood by the broadcasts on Shell and Exxon, isn't the only network accused of badgering businessmen and stacking the deck against them. Similar charges have been made against CBS's "60 Minutes" and ABC's "20/20" magazine shows.

Television's most watched program, "60 Minutes," has featured reporters Mike Wallace, Morley Safer, Dan Rather, and Harry Reasoner tracking down greedy businessmen, bungling bureaucrats and assorted other bad guys. This strikes some detractors as catering to populist fears and prejudices, but to the "60 Minutes" team it is just good journalism, clean fun, and lively viewing. Most of the greedy businessmen "60 Minutes" goes after are minor con men peddling worthless desert real estate, mail-order diplomas, "miracle" cancer cures, and the like. But "60 Minutes" also has taken on big business, criticizing General Foods Corporation and other food processors for overloading their products with sugar, scoring cotton manufacturers for failing to protect their mill employees from lung-damaging cotton dust, and going after pesticide makers for poisoning rivers, wells, and their own workers.

Some businessmen have accused "60 Minutes" correspondents of trying to entrap them. But what they call entrapment is generally only confrontation. An example: In investigating fraudulently upgraded beef sold at inflated prices, Dan Rather confronted a San Diego meat packing executive, showing him a phony rubber stamp his firm used to misbrand beef. "Boy, oh boy, what a disgusting deal!" the executive complained, walking away.

Don Hewitt, executive producer of "60 Minutes," has defended such confrontation tactics. "Anyone is fair game in an interview situation in his area of expertise," he said. "No one has to talk." Hewitt also has defended "60 Minutes" against charges that it is antibusiness, pointing out that many pieces, although less memorable than the critical ones, have put business in a favorable light. These include a piece sympathetic to an open-shop building contractor harassed by construction unions, a puffish profile of Mary Kay Cosmetics Inc., and a piece on businessmen buried by unnecessary paperwork imposed by the government.

Some critics have charged "60 Minutes" with using gratuitous scare tactics in showing victims of corporate policies that favor profits over people. Cotton mill workers coughing and wheezing from "brown lung," pesticide workers with nervous tremors and even paralysis, and the painfully burned faces of passengers in Pintos whose poorly placed gasoline tanks caused fires in rear-end crashes may make unpleasant viewing, but they do provide visible, incontrovertible evidence that something happened and are anything but gratuitous.

"60 Minutes" slips up, of course. It made two major errors in a 1979 piece on cost overruns at an Illinois nuclear plant under construction, and later corrected the errors on the air. Just as bad, to support its thesis that Illinois Power Company had mismanaged the project, causing construction to take much longer and cost much more than planned, "60 Minutes" used several of the utility's former employees despite their suspect credibility.

There have been sins of omission as well. For instance, "60 Minutes" failed to follow up its 1977 report on sugary food by reporting that a California court had dismissed a lawsuit prominently mentioned in the report. The suit charged General Foods with deceptively advertising its sugar-coated breakfast cereals as nutritious. Said executive producer Hewitt of the court action: "We probably should have mentioned it."

Corporation Countermeasures against TV

Corporations generally don't help their own cause by clamming up when reporters from "60 Minutes" and other news programs come by. Several department store chains selling clothes made by illegal aliens who are paid less than the minimum wage practically invited damage to their reputations by turning down interviews for a "60 Minutes" piece on garment sweat shops.

Some companies play favorites. After joining Chrysler as chairman, Lee A. Iacocca turned down hundreds of interview requests, including one from ABC economics editor Cordtz, while granting an interview to ABC's Barbara Walters. Said Cordtz: "He was smart enough to know I would do a tougher interview with him than Barbara; besides, there is a cachet about being interviewed by Barbara Walters."

Many companies deny access to their plants as well as their executives. Chrysler gave ABC permission to film its modern auto assembly plant in Belvidere, Ill., but not its grimy Detroit factories. Dow

Chemical Company wouldn't allow public TV to film the manufacture of the controversial herbicide 2,4,5-T for a documentary called "A Plague on Our Children."

Some corporations impose conditions on their cooperation. Mobil has grown so accustomed to controlling the format and content of the weekly opinion ads it has been running in newspapers for years that it frequently rejects television interviews it can't edit and refuses to participate in panel discussions that offer it only a few minutes to present its case. A number of oil producers have turned down invitations to participate in panel discussions because they didn't want to debate industry critics or enhance the critics' credibility. Some have relented only after the producer threatened to leave an empty chair on the set and read off the names of companies refusing to appear.

Some companies won't even reply to direct criticism. When San Francisco TV station KRON aired "Politics of Poison," a documentary critical of the aerial spraying of herbicides manufactured by Dow Chemical and others, it offered Dow rebuttal time following the documentary. But, as a Dow spokesman put it, "We declined to appear and in one or two minutes explain what was incorrect in a one-hour emotional circus."

Although a minute or two seems inadequate for a detailed rebuttal, it is a lot more than most people, including business critics, get on TV. As an example, NBC correspondent Michael Jensen and a crew of three invested a full day on an interview with radical economist Samuel Bowles at the University of Massachusetts at Amherst, only to use only 49 of Bowles's words on the evening news.

Said Jensen: "He got the same 20 seconds as anyone else." Government officials are also cut short.
For its piece on fraudulently upgraded beef, "60
Minutes" slashed an interview with Assistant Secretary of Agriculture Carol Tucker Foreman to a
mere six words.

With air time at such a premium, businessmen
who can organize their thoughts well and summa-
rize their positions concisely stand the best chance
of surviving severe editing. To help corporate executives think quickly on their feet, articulate brief
answers to complicated and sometimes unfriendly
questions, and to appear at ease before TV lights,
cameras, and microphones, the U.S. Chamber of
Commerce and other groups now sponsor workshops at which executives participate in mock TV
interviews. The interviews are videotaped and cri-
tiqued so the businessmen can see themselves as
others see them.

A growing number of major corporations are
videotaping actual television interviews with their
executives so that they have a record of what was
said and can compare it with what appears on the
air. Exxon's and Shell Oil's recordings of their
executives' interviews with NBC provided evidence
of the crucial rebuttal that NBC left out. Fortunately for the reputations of both business and
broadcasting, distortions as egregious as the NBC
report on Shell are the exception.

Perhaps business's biggest gripe against TV is the
routine refusal of all three networks to give or even
sell air time to corporations like Exxon and Shell
to reply to damaging coverage. Even though some
TV newsmen believe the practice is journalistically
unjustified, the networks defend it in specific cases

by saying that their news reports are fair and accurate, and rebuttal is therefore unnecessary and inappropriate.

It also is journalistically unjustified for television to expect cooperation and candor from other businesses while remaining close-mouthed about its own business. TV probes price increases in fuel, food, and other consumer essentials but, in common with newspapers, it rarely mentions the sharp runup in its own prices—the rates it charges advertisers. This isn't because ad rate increases are insignificant. National advertisers paying more than $150,000 for 30 seconds of time on top-rated "60 Minutes" routinely pass their higher ad costs on to consumers in the form of higher prices, worsening inflation.

On the other hand, businesses with something to hide can be thankful that the networks' bottom-line considerations have all but dried up full-length investigative documentaries. Why carry on in the tradition of such muckraking classics as "Harvest of Shame," the 1960 CBS documentary about corporate exploitation of migrant farm labor, and "You and the Commercial," the 1973 CBS documentary about TV advertisers' manipulation of consumers, when audiences for such fare are limited, advertisers are indifferent and the industries criticized will only be livid? It is only when an industry calls attention to itself by generating unusually unfavorable news that television feels obligated to scrutinize it. Nuclear power became just such an industry after a single incident in Pennsylvania in 1979.

5

Nuclear Power: A Free Ride until TMI

Two weeks before the March 1979 nuclear accident at Three Mile Island, the nearby *York* (Pa.) *Daily Record* published a series of articles citing serious safety hazards at the plant and warning that a major nuclear accident there could kill several thousand people and devastate much of York County.

"Fantasy," charged the head of the utility operating Three Mile Island. Suggesting that the plant be shut down to protect lives and property is "tantamount to yelling 'fire' in a crowded theater when there is no fire," Walter Creitz, president of Metropolitan Edison Company, said in a letter to the *York Daily Record* that was published just two days before Met Ed's reactor went awry.

Creitz was correct that the worst scenario envisioned by the government and antinuclear scientists quoted by reporter Jim Hill didn't materialize. But the nuclear accident that did take place was serious enough to cause an estimated $1 billion in damage and additional billions in power-replacement costs, to force the plant's shutdown for at least five years, and to call the future of U.S. nuclear power into question.

Metropolitan Edison's Creitz is far from alone in accusing the news media of antinuclear bias. The Atomic Industrial Forum, whose members include nuclear utilities and reactor suppliers, thinks the press has long kept the nuclear controversy alive with one-sided, exaggerated coverage. Said Carl Goldstein, AIF assistant vice president for media relations: "Nuclear power is a symbol or token of just about every presumed threat to society—big business, high technology, mysterious and arrogant science. It's a natural target for the new breed of passionate, brash, involved, and often careless reporter."

Media Coverage before TMI

Be that as it may, until Three Mile Island forced the press to focus attention on nuclear power, few reporters took much notice of it and fewer still were critical of it. Consider television coverage. According to a study by the Media Institute, a business-funded research group, the three TV networks allotted nuclear news just one quarter of 1 percent of the time available for news on their evening newscasts between August 1968 and March 27, 1979, the day before the TMI accident. That worked out to an average of less than four seconds of nuclear news in each 22-minute newscast, hardly enough to give viewers much information or insight into the benefits and risks of nuclear power.

Local TV stations and newspapers, particularly in areas with controversial reactors, have provided more extensive coverage. But few local news organizations have shown much taste for hard digging.

Although the public records of the Nuclear Regulatory Commission are replete with reports of equipment failures, careless operating procedures, and other "incidents" at nuclear reactors, few reporters have bothered to dig them out. As a consequence, many incidents have gone unreported. For example, Southern Californians learned only years later that an experimental reactor near Santa Susana had sustained a partial fuel meltdown in 1959.

The press's generally uncritical coverage of nuclear power until Three Mile Island stemmed mainly from overreliance on, and excessive credence in, government and industry sources of information. For more than 20 years, government and industry scientists assured journalists that nuclear reactors were fail-safe, and for more than 20 years most journalists had neither the motivation nor the technical background to dispute them.

Antinuclear scientists were available, of course, but few reporters sought their guidance on either technology or public policy. During the more than 10 years of network television news studied by the Media Institute, the three most quoted nuclear critics—the Union of Concerned Scientists, Ralph Nader, and the National Resources Defense Council—accumulated a grand total of 12 minutes of network evening news time. (The three most quoted nongovernment nuclear proponents got a collective seven minutes.)

With some notable exceptions, such as the consistently antinuclear *St. Louis Post-Dispatch,* newspapers before Three Mile Island generally welcomed nuclear projects as major props to their local economies. For instance, when the Tennessee Valley Authority's Browns Ferry nuclear plant in

Alabama was heavily damaged by fire in 1975, nuclear critics questioned the TVA's competence in nuclear management and urged a halt to its nuclear building program. But most newspapers in the area, both in editorials and in letters to the Nuclear Regulatory Commission, supported the prompt reopening of the plant.

The nuclear industry's success in winning journalists' appreciation of nuclear technology stems partly from its organized tours of nuclear facilities. The Atomic Industrial Forum has sponsored half a dozen such press tours. Reporters going on them are free to write what they wish, but most send back glowing reports.

An AIF-organized tour for 17 American journalists of nuclear facilities in the Soviet Union in 1978 produced a flurry of stories emphasizing the Soviet commitment to breeder technology and plutonium fuel, and contrasting it with the United States's more cautious and equivocal development of nuclear power. *Time* magazine introduced its account: "While perfervid demonstrators, dallying bureaucrats and well-paid lawyers are holding back the development of U.S. atomic power, the U.S.S.R. is moving ahead rapidly with its own nuclear programs."

The TMI Tocsin   Many American journalists remained high on nukes and down on their detractors right up to Three Mile Island. For instance, George F. Will devoted his column in the issue of *Newsweek* on sale when the TMI reactor malfunctioned to a denunciation of Jane Fonda's just-released film, *The China Syndrome.* The movie "rests on fantasy rather than fact," Will sniffed, and strives "to manipulate audiences into antinuclear hysteria." Just how wrong Will was became obvious to viewers of ABC's "20/20" magazine show three weeks later when "20/20" alternated scenes from the fictional melodrama with newsfilm of the real-life melodrama. "20/20"'s conclusion: "Some of the parallels between the movie and the events in Pennsylvania are almost too close for comfort."

Like the TV reporter that Jane Fonda played in the movie, the reporters who swarmed into Harrisburg were as unprepared to cover a nuclear accident as Metropolitan Edison and the Nuclear Regulatory Agency were to explain it. "At the beginging, at least, the vast majority of reporters had no idea what anybody was talking about. Anchorless on a sea of rads and rems and roentgens, of core vessels and containments and cooling systems, they built their stories around the discrepancies between sources," two on-the-spot observers for the *Columbia Journalism Review* reported. "What is surprising about the TMI coverage that emerged is not that it was sometimes technically wrong, but that it was so often technically right," the observers, Peter M. Sandman and Mary Paden, concluded.

Accurate coverage was hampered by contradictory and inaccurate statements from official sources. For instance, on the morning of the first day of the accident, while Met Ed president Creitz was telling reporters of the release of some radiation, the utility's public relations officials were telling other reporters that no radiation had been released.

Bill Gross, a Met Ed public relations official, later defended the utility's information as "straightforward and factual. There was no deliberate attempt to tell it other than it was." Gross blamed the credibility gap that developed soon after reporters arrived at TMI on their "built-in Watergate mentality—a general feeling of distrust of big business and big government. We may have had two strikes against us when they came in."

However, he and other utility officials seem to be almost alone in their high opinion of their performance. The special presidential commission that investigated the TMI accident concluded: "While there is no unambiguous evidence of cover-up, some utility officials showed a marked capacity for self-deception, and others hid behind technical jargon to obscure answers to troublesome questions."

A Divergence of Perspectives

Nuclear defenders like to point out that no one was killed or even hurt at Three Mile Island. Indeed, according to the Atomic Industrial Forum, the accident "had less of a public health and safety impact than many industrial accidents that occurred in the country that week." Yet the news media devoted considerably more space and time to TMI than to fatal accidents elsewhere. Was this justified? Nuclear defenders say no. Journalists say yes.

"To stress that no one died begs the question," according to Peter Stoler, who covered TMI for *Time* magazine. "The fact that it almost happened shows that something is wrong. The story was that this plant came more than half-way to meltdown, and that's too close. The unthinkable has occurred."

Inevitably, a few journalists went overboard. Jimmy Breslin of the New York *Daily News* reported seeing "evil" steam "laced with radiation" that "drifted out of the tops of the four cooling towers and ran down the sides like candle wax." Many reporters played up the suspicions of TMI-area farmers that radiation from the reactor was killing their cows and goats, without giving equal prominence to follow-up reports that the deaths were actually from mundane causes unconnected to radiation.

But on the whole, newspapers and broadcasters, especially those in Pennsylvania, made an effort to downplay danger so as not to panic the public. A study conducted for the presidential commission found that of 43 newspapers only two tabloids, the *New York Post* and to a lesser extent the New York *Daily News,* were guilty of sensationalism. Among the *Post's* offending headlines: "NUKE LEAK GOES OUT OF CONTROL" and "RACE WITH NUCLEAR DISASTER."

The study, conducted by researchers headed by New York University journalism professor David M. Rubin, concluded: "While the media can be criticized for missing some stories and failing to provide a context for others, they were generally not guilty of the most common criticism leveled at them: that they presented an overwhelmingly alarming view of the accident."

By the nuclear industry's lights, of course, the media have been alarming the public for years. The Atomic Industrial Forum dates alarmist coverage from about 1970 when nuclear energy became "the most visible and convenient target of the environmental, antigrowth movement." The AIF contends that since 1970, television documentaries and magazine-show segments critical of nuclear power have significantly outnumbered favorable ones. Indeed, it can think of only three documentaries—a 1977 CBS three-hour special on energy, a 1977 ABC special, "Nuclear Power: Pro and Con," and a 1979 public TV special, "Do I Look Like I Want to Die?"—that were fair to the nuclear industry.

Antinuclear documentaries that have particularly upset the AIF include NBC's "Danger: Radioactive Waste," CBS's "Fallout from Three Mile Island," and three public TV specials, "Plutonium: Element of Risk," "Incident at Browns Ferry," and "Paul Jacobs and the Nuclear Gang."

Not content to take its lumps in silence, the Atomic Industrial Forum has made a practice of firing off long, detailed letters of complaint to network and public TV officials. And in the case of NBC's "Danger: Radioactive Waste," it and other nuclear industry groups took a complaint to the National News Council. In an 18-page decision, the independent media-monitoring group rejected the complainants' allegations that "Danger: Radioactive Waste" was biased, unbalanced, and lacked perspective. But the council found the documentary "seriously flared" in implying without evidence that radiation had sickened cattle near a nuclear waste dump in Kentucky and had caused genetic damage to two deformed sons of a former nuclear worker. This smacked of "scare tactics," the council agreed.

Some of the Atomic Industrial Forum's objections to other documentaries also have been valid. For instance, CBS in "Fallout from Three Mile Island" used an anonymous, unanswered charge that TVA's Browns Ferry plant had stood on the brink of a meltdown. And the network failed to identify physicist Henry Kendall as an official of the antinuclear Union of Concerned Scientists.

However, many of the factual errors that AIF has cited in its letters of complaint seem minor or are actually matters of opinion, interpretation, and emphasis. Take the question of what the radioactive material that is returned from foreign reactors built with U.S. help should be termed. In a segment on how the United States is becoming a "nuclear dumping ground," "20/20" called the returned material "waste." But the AIF insists that it is "spent fuel" destined to be reprocessed into uranium and plutonium, with only a small part of what remains requiring disposal. However, even the small amount of waste remaining after reprocessing is highly toxic, and permanent dumps where it can be disposed of safely are still unavailable.

The Atomic Industrial Forum has quibbled over the style as well as the substance of TV documentaries. It has criticized several documentaries for using visual tricks and sound effects to make nuclear plants appear menacing. For instance, NBC's "Danger: Radioactive Waste" made nuclear plants appear to give off colored waves, and its background sound effects included the click of a geiger counter and the score of *The Sorcerer's Apprentice.* However, a certain amount of theatricality seems pardonable in a predominately entertainment medium in which hype is rife and channel switching routine. As producer Robert Richter said of his use of background electronic music and the ominous hum of high-tension power lines in "Incident at Browns Ferry": "I plead justifiable accenting to keep the audience's interest."

The Atomic Industrial Forum claims that "Incident at Browns Ferry" and some other documentaries have been so transparently biased against nuclear energy that they should have been preceded by warnings to the audience. Before "Paul Jacobs

and the Nuclear Gang" was shown on public TV,
the AIF pressed Public Broadcasting Service to add
a disclaimer that the documentary was "a personal
point of view not necessarily supported by the
known facts or endorsed by PBS." PBS didn't go
along.

To the AIF, just about everything about "Paul
Jacobs and the Nuclear Gang" was propagandistic,
starting with the title, which suggested that the
Army, the old Atomic Energy Commission and the
civilian nuclear industry acted like a bunch of thugs
in exposing Americans to hazardous doses of radiation, and then denied responsibility and covered
up. The script was propagandistic, according to the
AIF, in contending that low-level radiation caused
a high incidence of cancer among soldiers exposed
to nuclear weapons tests in Nevada, as well as to
civilians living in Southern Utah downwind of the
test site, civilians living near the nuclear weapons
plant at Rocky Flats, Colo., and workers at the
Portsmouth, N.H., naval shipyard, which builds
nuclear-powered submarines.

However, what seems most remarkable about
"Paul Jacobs and the Nuclear Gang" is the matter-
of-fact way it presented its case and the unemo-
tional interviews it conducted with victims of cancer attributed to radiation. Among these cancer
victims was reporter Paul Jacobs, first exposed to
nuclear radiation while investigating the Nevada
bomb tests in 1957. Along with three others interviewed on the documentary, Jacobs died shortly
after it was filmed. Producer Jack Willis conceded
that the documentary presented "a one-sided argument," but said "we did it to redress the imbalance
of 20 years of the press reporting the government's
and the industry's side of the argument."

David Loxton, head of the independent documentary unit at WNET-TV in New York, which accepted "Paul Jacobs and the Nuclear Gang" for public TV, has defended the right of documentary makers like Jack Willis to express themselves. "Most journalism has a strong point of view, either explicit or implicit, and to pretend otherwise is crazy," he said. "A TV documentary is the equivalent of a bylined magazine article. Each and every documentary need not be objective and balanced, so long as there is balance over a period of time."

The National News Council agreed. In ruling on NBC's "Danger: Radioactive Waste," it declared: "What is essential in a documentary is that its conclusions be based on verifiable information—that is, on documentation—and not that it be fully objective. A major function of journalism is responsible interpretation."

A one-sided documentary can even present a truer picture than a scrupulously balanced, seemingly objective documentary. Take "Nuclear Power: Pro and Con," a 1977 ABC documentary that was divided evenly into arguments for and against nuclear power. Jules Bergman, who reported the pro-nuclear side, admitted later that the documentary was seriously flawed because "I didn't ask as many hard questions as I should have," naively "believing the utility companies and the NRC at face value."

It seems reasonable to conclude that the nuclear industry has mostly itself to blame for its post-TMI lack of credibility with journalists like Jules Bergman. Its reassurances about the safety of nuclear power have backfired, yet it continues to insist that low-level radiation has yet to be proved hazardous, a contention that reminds many journalists of the

tobacco industry's claim that evidence linking cigarette smoking to lung cancer is circumstantial
only. What's more, the nuclear industry's quickness
to complain about critical coverage indicates continued defensiveness. As one nuclear scientist has
put it, "I think they doth protest too much."

6

Reporting the Bottom Line

If there is one industry that ought to be grateful for the private enterprise system, it's the news business. Not only does it enjoy unique First Amendment privileges and immunities, but it is near the top of all industries in profitability. Daily newspapers keep up to a quarter of every dollar they take in, even after taxes. *Time* and *Newsweek* magazines are gold mines. And television, which has been likened to "a license to print money," is so lucrative that it bestows corporate presidents' salaries on many of its journalists.

With so much prosperity, it's little wonder that most journalists, especially high-salaried TV network journalists, know which side their bread is buttered on. "I believe in the profit system," said Paul Greenberg, executive producer of "NBC Nightly News," and "this company is built on the profit system." Added Don Hewitt, executive producer of CBS's "60 Minutes": "We're all capitalists here."

Be that as it may, journalists have been coming under increasing criticism for baiting the system that feeds them—more specifically, for treating corporate profits as though they were ill-gotten gains rather than essential grease keeping the economy humming. Oil companies complain that the news media have reported soaring oil profits unsympathetically and out of context, while all but ignoring the media's own embarrassment of riches. And businessmen of all stripes gripe that the media have failed to educate politicians and the public that far from being too high, profits need to go still higher to spur capital investment, create jobs, and reduce inflation.

Despite such business complaints, a close look at profit-reporting practices indicates that the news media's most serious shortcoming is not that they report profits unsympathetically but that they do so simplistically. Too many journalists accept the illusory precision of corporate financial statements at face value. Too few question the accounting conventions that enable companies to report high profits to investors and the public, while at the same time reporting lower profits to the tax collector.

As Harold M. Williams, chairman of the Securities and Exchange Commission, noted: "Conflicting reports of record profits on the one hand and inadequate earnings to maintain and expand capacity on the other, serve only to confuse the public and political leaders. Further, they raise questions about the integrity of financial reporting. Unfortunately, daily press reports of record earnings fail to communicate the effects of changing prices in a meaningful way, and thus the confusion and conflicting claims are likely to continue. In such a conflict, business, serving up the weapons for its own destruction, is clearly and predictably the loser."

Where Profits Lie   The first problem journalists encounter in reporting corporate profits is that the word *profit* never appears in corporate financial statements. Companies and their accountants prefer the technical term *net income.*

Arriving at net income seems straightforward enough. Take sales and other revenues, subtract payments for raw materials, wages, interest owed on debt, taxes and other expenses, as well as depreciation allowances, and what's left is net income. But it isn't so simple. There are so many ways to account for expenses and to calculate net income that many experts feel it is misleading for any company to report just one net income figure. "We do ourselves a disservice by printing one number and calling it net income," according to University of Chicago accounting professor Roman L. Weil. "We should print three, five, ten such numbers.

Corporations generally choose high net income numbers to report to their stockholders and the public. And it's easy to see why. Corporate executives whose standing and incentive compensation depend on their company's profit performance have a self-interest in plumping up profits. In addition, healthy profits help keep stock prices up, discouraging unwelcome takeover bids. This leads to temptations. In the 1970s, the SEC cited scores of companies, big and small, for overstating profits by misusing one accounting device or another.

It is perfectly legal for companies to report lower profits to the Internal Revenue Service than they do to their stockholders and the public. One of the ways companies do this is to take accelerated depreciation for tax purposes, while continuing to use straight-line depreciation in figuring the net income they report publicly.

Whereas straight-line depreciation involves uniform annual depreciation charges, accelerated depreciation allows a company to write off a piece of equipment in fewer years, or to take larger write-offs in the first few years than in the last few, or both. Since depreciation is a deductible, if non-cash, expense, the effect of using accelerated depreciation is to reduce taxable income below what's reported under straight-line depreciation to stockholders and the public.

Besides sheltering some corporate profits from taxes, depreciation write-offs are designed to allow a company to build up reserves to pay for replacing worn-down plant and equipment. However, since depreciation write-offs are based on what a company originally paid for plant and equipment, they may not cover replacement costs in this period of double-digit inflation.

Businessmen cite this in arguing that depreciation allowances are inadequate and that they need still higher profits to build up still bigger reserves for replacing plant and equipment. What they—and the media—seldom point out is that as bookkeeping deductions representing no cash outlay, depreciation write-offs make more money available for current use in the business or for any type of investment, and need not actually be used to replace old facilities.

Inflation also affects inventory accounting. Companies valuing their goods in inventory at acquisition cost rather than replacement cost show a one-shot profit from the increase in value between the time the goods were originally purchased and when they are sold. But to remain in business, these companies have to replace these inventories at higher prices, so this profit is largely illusory.

Companies can reduce illusory inventory profits by basing the cost of goods sold on the price of the last item added to inventory. But most companies prefer to base the cost of goods sold on the price of the first item added to inventory. This overstates profits and unnecessarily increases taxes, but it also keeps up the illusion of higher profts.

The Media and Corporation Reports

Newspapers report these overstated profits at face value and unsophisticated investors are taken in by them. But sophisticated money managers for banks, mutual funds, and other institutional investors subscribe to services such as the twice-monthly *Quality of Earnings Report* to keep them apprised of accounting conventions' effects on real profits. Meanwhile, the stock market isn't fooled, as demonstrated by the failure of common stock prices to keep up with inflation in the 1970s.

Newspapers can be faulted for failing to issue general alerts that corporate profit figures are unreliable. But they can hardly be blamed for failing to correct the figures that individual corporations report. There simply are too many corporations, their accounting practices are too complex, and they all tend to report their financial results at about the same time, flooding newspaper offices a few weeks after the close of each calendar quarter with news releases that typically are thick and difficult to digest—and sometimes are less than straightforward.

Consider MCA Inc.'s news release on third-quarter 1979 results. It began by boasting that profits were the second highest for any third quarter in the company's history, obscuring the fact, as noted later in the news release, that profits actually fell 12 percent from the year before.

Or take the way General Motors Corporation reported its third-quarter 1979 results. Its news release reported a $21 million profit for the quarter without mentioning that operations actually resulted in a loss of nearly $100 million. The operating loss could be inferred from an item on GM's income statement sent shareholders and attached to news releases provided some reporters, but it wasn't obvious. Most newspapers missed it, reporting only that GM was still in the black.

Roger B. Smith, then executive vice president of GM, said neither the operating loss nor the reduction in income-tax reserves from which the loss could be inferred was included in the news release because "we didn't think it important." However, many reporters and Wall Street security analysts concluded GM was simply trying to hide its first operating loss in nine years.

Oil companies have attributed startling gains in their profits primarily to foreign operations, but critics of the industry and some journalists have suggested that the oil companies have doctored their books to overstate foreign income and understate U.S. income. The object: to minimize both U.S. taxes and criticism that they're fattening off American motorists' misery.

Reporters have discovered that it's a lot easier to generalize about oil industry bookkeeping manipulation than to prove any individual company guilty of it. A *New York Times* story charging oil companies with deriving "hundreds of millions of dollars in foreign profits . . . from petroleum products ultimately sold in the United States" seemed persuasive, but one of the companies named, Exxon Corporation, complained that the story was "wrong in detail and misleading overall."

Mobil Corporation took even stronger exception to a "CBS Evening News" story on oil profits and bookkeeping gimmickry. Although the story did not specifically accuse Mobil of earning "a foreign profit from an American consumer," correspondent Ray Brady clearly implicated Mobil by concluding his general accusations posed in front of a Mobil filling station sign.

Mobil vehemently denied the implication, taking two-page ads in a dozen newspapers to point out that the "whimsical scheme" CBS described was forbidden by U.S. tax law and price control regulations. Mobil asked for air time to correct "the erroneous impression" left by the broadcast, but CBS, standing by its story, rejected the request. This struck even journalists as high-handed and unfair, given the network's exclusion of oil industry comment from its one-sided story and the seriousness of its charges.

Reporters also have run into problems with government data on corporate profits. When the Commerce Department estimates corporate profits each quarter, its news releases contain dollar estimates, but not quarter-to-quarter or year-to-year percentage changes. Reporters must calculate the percentage changes on their own or ask Commerce Department economists to do it for them. And this leaves room for error.

In reporting Commerce Department profit data in March 1979, a number of news organizations, including the Associated Press and the *Washington Post,* incorrectly put the jump in 1978 profits over 1977 at 26.4 percent, instead of the actual 16.2 percent. And others, including the *Los Angeles Times* and the *Washington Post,* took the rate of profit increase between the third and fourth quarters of 1978 and projected it forward for an entire year. With compounding, this resulted in a whopping 44.8 percent annual profit gain. Commerce Department economist Kenneth Petrick felt the projection was inappropriate because profits are notoriously volatile, but he himself provided the projection for reporters who requested it.

The inflated profit reports helped inflame the national debate then raging over high corporate profits and prices. White House inflation fighter Alfred E. Kahn said the profit gains strengthened "the widespread belief that many American businesses aren't assuming their full responsibility to fight inflation." And George Meany, president of the AFL–CIO, called the figures "the grossest demonstration of profit-gouging since the opening days of the Korean War."

But Heath Larry, president of the National Association of Manufacturers, argued that even heftier profit increases were necessary to make up deficiencies in depreciation reserves caused by inflation. "The inflation problem is not that profits have been rising too fast," he said, "but that they have not been rising fast enough."

Ironically, considering the furor the profit estimates caused and the partisan uses to which they were put, the Commerce Department subsequently revised its estimate of the increase in fourth-quarter 1978 profits downward from an after-tax 9.6 percent to a modest 6.2 percent over the third quarter. This got no media attention, but nonetheless provided another example of the folly of taking precise but frequently unreliable statistics too seriously.

To their credit, journalists have treated the Commerce Department's profit estimates more carefully and skeptically since the 1979 fiasco. But this hasn't stilled business complaints that the news media continue to overplay profit gains that feed public misconceptions about widespread profiteering.

Some businessmen blame business itself for playing up hefty year-to-year profit gains in their news releases rather than more meaningful measures such as profit margin, return on stockholders' equity, and return on invested capital. Some companies have begun rectifying this by emphasizing their profit margin (net income as a percentage of sales and other revenues).

Oil producers have attempted to deflect attention from their spectacular profit gains by stressing that their return on stockholders' equity is in line with the average for all U.S. manufacturers. However, return on stockholders' equity (annual net income as a percentage of the par value of common stock, plus surplus capital and retained earnings) can also be misleading. *Business Week,* for one, has asserted that return on stockholders' equity has been "distorted almost beyond usefulness" because inflation has puffed up both net income and retained earnings.

Most experts agree that the most reliable indicator of profitability is return on total capital (annual net income as a percentage of stockholders' equity plus borrowed funds). But few companies mention return on capital in their news releases, and reporters understandably fear to calculate it on their own lest they make a mistake.

High Profits for the News Media

By any measure of profitability, the news media shine. According to *Forbes* magazine's annual study of profits, broadcasting and publishing companies led all industry groups in return on both stockholders' equity and capital in 1975-79. In 1978, Gannett Company's 78 dailies had pretax profit margins ranging from 4 percent to an astounding 48 percent.

Major dailies such as the *Los Angeles Times, New York Times,* and *The Wall Street Journal* generally report their parent companies' profits as prominently as they report those of other companies of comparable size. And the *Des Moines Register* discloses its parent company's profits even though the parent company is closely held and isn't obligated to make its profits public. But these seem to be the exceptions. Most newspapers have little or nothing to say about how much money they make. And television is even less forthright. CBS's "60 Minutes" mentioned the three networks' profits in a 1978 story on TV programming, but network newscasts rarely if ever have. The explanation: Air time is tight and TV profits are less important than the profits of oil, auto, and other industries with more impact on the economy.

While it's understandable that many businessmen are envious of the media's riches, they have little cause to plead poverty themselves. True, corporate profitability has declined from its peak in the mid-

1960s, but it still compares favorably with that of the 1950s when calculated on total capital invested. As companies have increasingly financed expansion by borrowing from banks rather than issuing new stock, returns have shifted from stockholders to lenders, but total returns to all investors have held up fairly well.

In any event, business worries about public attitudes toward profits seem misplaced. As Louis B. Lundborg, retired chairman of Bank of America, has noted: "It is not profits as such; it is the feeling that business does not care about anything *but* profits" that disturbs Americans. Eric A. Weiss, public issues analyst for Sun Company, the oil producer, agrees. "The public is far less concerned about the level of corporate profits than it is about corporate misuse of power, corporate secrecy, corporate failure to protect the environment and the health and safety of employees, and corporate failure to provide good products at a fair price."

7

Uncovering
Environmental
Hazards

The skilled craftsmen who build full-scale wood
models of automobiles for design purposes are
used to their smelly, dusty workshops—but not to
their shopmates dying of cancer. So when the
fourth model maker at one of General Motors
Corporation's suburban Detroit model shops was
buried a cancer victim in 1979, worried shopmates
got in touch with the *Detroit News.*

Reporter Douglas Ilka interviewed the families
of cancer victims, conferred with experts on workplace health hazards, checked death certificates,
and managed to confirm eight cancer deaths and
seven other cancer cases among the 400 GM Fisher
Body Division model makers. Embarrassed by these
grim facts in a series of articles Ilka wrote, General
Motors dispatched three officials to the *Detroit
News*'s offices to complain it was irresponsibly
frightening GM employees. Chairman Thomas A.
Murphy followed up with a letter denouncing the
daily for "creating hysteria and anxiety before the
facts are known."

The *Detroit News* series on cancer at General Motors points up the progress and the perils of the news media's increasing attention to workplace health hazards and other environmental dangers. More enterprising than they used to be in alerting the public to environmental contamination, journalists nonetheless continue to be confronted with imprecise data and conflicting interpretations among technical experts that make it difficult to establish the cause and severity of environmental problems. And environmental coverage is further complicated by the press's responsibility to avoid unnecessarily alarming workers whose jobs as well as health may be at stake, and to avoid unfairly creating economic hardships for businesses and even entire industries.

Stepping on Business's Toes

Although environmental coverage is less scattershot and more sophisticated than it used to be, it still isn't careful enough to suit industry. Many corporations are quick to denounce messengers bearing news of the mess. Some companies have reacted defensively to even the most thoroughly researched and evenly balanced accounts, while holding the news media generally guilty of exaggerating environmental dangers, giving emotional laymen more credence than technical experts, and helping destroy the public's trust in technology.

Examining the media's performance on half a dozen significant environmental stories—dumping at Love Canal, uranium mining hazards, the herbicide 2,4,5-T, a cancer scare involving Xerox copiers, and the GM cancer controversy—spotlights both the successes and shortcomings of environmental reporting.

Like GM, many corporations whose environmental practices are portrayed unflatteringly have struck back at the press with angry letters, point-by-point rebuttals, news releases, and paid ads. Some alleged polluters have even turned the tables on their tormentors by accusing journalists of contributing to environmental problems. For instance, Johns-Manville Corporation has charged that the press has helped send asbestos workers to early graves by not warning that smoking cigarettes greatly increases their chances of contracting lung cancer.

The pillorying that Johns-Manville and other companies contend they're getting in the press contrasts with the nearly free ride they used to get in the 1950s and 1960s when pollution proceeded with little notice except from a handful of conservation magazines. Even the *National Geographic* was slow to identify and investigate environmental damage, not devoting a major article to it until 1970. Some news organizations were openly hostile to environmentalists in those days. When Rachel Carson published *Silent Spring* in 1962, *Time* magazine dismissed this seminal critique of pesticides as an "emotional and inaccurate outburst" full of "scary generalizations" that were "patently unsound."

By the late 1960s, however, foul air in the cities, inflammable scum on industrial rivers, oil spills on ocean beaches, and congestion most everywhere were all too apparent to everyone. Even journalists could see, smell, and taste the problem. The Santa Barbara oil well blowout of 1969 generated extensive national coverage, and Earth Day 1970 prompted lengthy appraisals of the environmental malaise.

Nowadays, small and medium-size newspapers

typically give the increasingly complex, sprawling environmental beat haphazard, piecemeal coverage. Most metropolitan newspapers assign a specialist or two to it, and some use other reporters as needed to help prepare such major investigations as the *Los Angeles Times*'s 1979-1980 series, "The Poisoning of America." More noteworthy, papers in some industry-dominated cities and states are finally growing skeptical of industry information and assurances and are starting to look into the environmental hazards of industrial workplaces and development projects.

The *Charlotte Observer* in 1980 devoted an eight-part series of articles to byssinosis, the crippling cotton-dust disease that threatens the lungs and even the lives of the 115,000 Carolinas mill workers who turn out the nation's towels, sheets, and jeans. The series showed how most textile companies have fought efforts to solve the problem and help afflicted workers, and how state agencies have failed to force the mills to clean up.

The *Louisville Courier-Journal* showed similar enterprise in conducting a six-month investigation of improper toxic waste disposal in Kentucky and Indiana. A *Courier-Journal* reporter posing as a toxic waste hauler drove a pickup truck with empty drums stenciled with the names of such deadly toxins as dioxin to 14 dumps, none of which was legally permitted to accept such hazardous substances but only one of which turned him away.

The Love Canal story received nationwide attention after another reporter showed similar initiative. To check complaints from homeowners living near the Niagara Falls dump that long-buried wastes were oozing from the canal into their basements and sickening their families, Michael Brown of the *Niagara Gazette* toured the neigborhood, filling jars with water from basement sump pumps. He had the water analyzed by a laboratory, which found the trace presence of a number of chemicals buried in the canal itself. "It turned out that the situation was much worse than county and state officials had acknowledged," Brown concluded.

Hooker Chemical Company disputes Brown's version of the situation and has included his reporting in its general accusation that "irresponsible journalism" has grossly overstated the seriousness of the Love Canal problem, "unjustly dragged Hooker through the mud," and "helped create much of the hysteria and emotionalism" among nearby residents, perhaps even causing some of the high number of miscarriages to pregnant women there.

Despite such sweeping charges against the news media, only in 1980 did Hooker begin to rebut specific coverage it considered inaccurate or unfair. And only in 1980 did it begin to open up and respond to reporters' requests for information and comment. Donald L. Baeder, Hooker's president, conceded that some of the bad press Hooker had received resulted from both its unresponsiveness and its failure to correct erroneous reports. "We thought we would have a quick blow in the media and then get our fair day in court," he explained. "But I think we are being tried in the media, and we finally decided we can't allow it to go unanswered."

Among the reports that Hooker now disputes is the implication that Love Canal was inappropriate as a toxic waste dump because it was in a position to poison Niagara Falls's drinking water supply. The company says dumping punctured drums of toxic chemical wastes a quarter mile from the Niagara River was consistent with "state of the art" technology at the time—1942 to 1953—and it is unfair of the media to judge such past practices by today's knowledge and standards.

Hooker also disputes press reports that much of the Love Canal vicinity was silty swampland that was conducive to the spread of contaminants. It says the ground was impervious clay that prevented chemicals from draining away. And it maintains that rather than escaping underground, toxic wastes were spread through the neighborhood when the city, after taking over the canal from Hooker in 1953, disturbed its clay covering, allowing rainwater to fill up the canal and make it overflow, and when some contaminated earth was used as landfill in the construction of streets.

Although three streets were built across the 78-yard wide canal property after Hooker deeded it to the city, no homes were built on it, as some careless news reports have stated. The only thing built on top of the canal itself was a paved playground, and it and an adjacent public school were in a section that had been used primarily for the dumping of municipal garbage, not chemical wastes.

Hooker's claim that it warned the city not to disturb chemical wastes buried in the canal got support when *The Wall Street Journal* published evidence that Hooker had warned Niagara Falls in 1957, four years after deeding it the canal, that the land was unsuitable for construction in which basements, sewers, and other underground facilities would be necessary. A few scattered newspapers picked up the evidence from the *Journal,* but most ignored it.

Other Hooker claims are harder to judge. Its contention that chemicals buried in the canal have hurt no one flies in the face of reports of a rash of serious illnesses, miscarriages, and birth defects among nearby residents, and a finding by government authorities of sufficient harm to warrant the evacuation of hundreds of families. However, New York State studies have found no direct evidence of a cause-effect relationship between chemicals from the canal and acute health problems. A chromosome study commissioned by the federal Environmental Protection Agency concluded that a third of the Love Canal residents tested showed genetic damage. But Hooker contended the study was scientifically flawed and "totally inadequate," and got support for that position from a panel of scientists appointed by New York State.

The chromosome study points up the awkward position that questionable government studies and official statements place reporters in. Should they stick to just reporting studies and statements they suspect are flawed, or should they go further and independently attempt to assess their validity? In the case of the chromosome study, most reporters followed the easiest and safest course, confining their coverage to the EPA's findings and Hooker's objections, and even Hooker didn't expect more than that. "The media did a very responsible, thorough, balanced job in reporting the chromosome study," a company spokesman said.

However, Hooker faults the media for focusing too heavily on the angry, anguished Love Canal residents. "The least credible person tends to get as much play in the press as responsible officials," company president Baeder complained, referring to leaders of the canal residents.

Baeder was even more critical of the "rather unethical job" he felt CBS's "60 Minutes" did in December 1979 on "The Hooker Memos." The memos in question were internal documents of Hooker and its parent company, Occidental Petroleum Corporation. One 1975 memo showed that the chief environmental engineer at Occidental's chemical plant at Lathrop, Calif., had warned an indifferent management that the plant was illegally contaminating ground water with pesticide wastes. Interrogated by "60 Minutes" correspondent Mike Wallace, Baeder attempted to explain away the memo, but the refusal of the environmental engineer to be interviewed and Baeder's refusal to direct him to talk left an impression of wrongdoing.

So did another Occidental memo, this one from 1978 discussing the pesticide DBCP, which the Lathrop plant had stopped making after it caused sterility in male production workers. Reading excerpts from the memo on the air, Mike Wallace came to a sentence in which one plant official suggested to another that the company resume manufacturing DBCP if projected profits comfortably exceeded anticipated legal claims for damaging the health of employees. Wallace read that sentence but not the next one, which specified that resumption of production depended on finding no "significant" risk to Occidental workers.

The memos that Wallace and other reporters have used to put Occidental and Hooker Chemical on the spot resulted not from any strenuous investigative effort but from Occidental's aborted at-

tempt to take over Mead Corporation in 1978. The
forest products concern successfully resisted, and
in the discovery stage of its suit to block the takeover, Mead obtained some 100,000 documents
from Occidental files. The documents, many of
which found their way into the hands of federal
regulators, congressional investigators, and media
reporters, indicated that Occidental and its Hooker
subsidiary had followed a pattern in California,
Michigan, New York, and Florida of not alerting
authorities that their plants were polluting the air
and water.

Another cause célèbre replete with damaging
documents, conflicting claims and high passions
involves uranium mining and milling in New Mexico
and the ABC documentary "The Uranium Factor."
When the documentary aired in 1980, it enraged
not only the uranium industry but also its supporters in the media. In Grants, N.M., which bills itself
as the nation's uranium capital, the *Daily Beacon*
lambasted "The Uranium Factor" as "sensational,
scary and slanderous," and accused ABC of "out-
rageous hypocrisy," "galling effrontery," and
"prostitution of professional ethics for profits." In
Albuquerque, the ABC affiliate, KOAT-TV, aired
the documentary but found it so objectionable it
donated its facilities for a locally produced pro-
industry rebuttal, "Uranium: Fact or Fiction?"

A detailed analysis of both the ABC documentary and the KOAT rebuttal, plus interviews with
persons involved in their production and with several key sources interviewed on the shows, leaves
the conclusion that "The Uranium Factor" was
indeed vulnerable to criticism in several regards.

In reporting how New Mexico authorities had
been lax in imposing environmental safeguards on

uranium mines and mills, the ABC documentary oversimplified the history of one particularly controversial mill project. It left the impression that state officials, bowing to pressure, had temporarily licensed the mill without proper environmental safeguards, when actually the officials had only authorized construction while specifying the environmental safeguards required for an operating license.

Then too, "The Uranium Factor" got carried away demonstrating uranium's hazards. To demonstrate radon, the radioactive gas given off by uranium ore that is a menace to underground miners, ABC showed a mine venting what it gave viewers to understand was radon. Radon was indeed present in the cloud of vapor spewing from the mine vent, but because radon is invisible what viewers actually saw was moisture in the vented air striking the outdoor chill.

The documentary also went overboard in dramatizing the dangers of the radioactive piles of uranium mill tailings that dot the Southwest landscape. A scene of four Navaho Indian children frolicking on one tailings pile illustrated the hazard, but showing the scene twice and calling the pile "a lethal playground" smacked of overstatement.

Despite these and other flaws, "The Uranium Factor" performed a valuable service in bringing to the nation's attention a seldom noted but significant facet of the nuclear power controversy. And it showed evenhandedness in being just as critical of government authorities for inadequately enforcing environmental and safety regulations as it was of uranium producers for insufficiently protecting their employees and the environment. It also gave industry spokesmen their say, and might have included more spokesmen had they been available. However, one major producer, United Nuclear Corporation, refused to be interviewed. Not surprisingly, it came off looking worse than another producer, Kerr-McGee Corporation, which cooperated with ABC.

TV documentaries on other environmental topics have also included comment from the industries involved. Consider three 1979 documentaries examining the controversial aerial spraying of the herbicide 2,4,5-T—"Politics of Poison," produced by KRON–TV in San Francisco, and the public TV specials "Serpent Fruits" and "A Plague on Our Children."

Despite industry complaints that too few industry representatives appeared in these documentaries, all three carefully included interviews with spokesmen for Dow Chemical Corporation, a leading 2,4,5-T manufacturer, as well as other herbicide proponents. However, "A Plague on Our Children" was remiss in not giving International Paper Company a chance to comment on an Oregon resident's passing reference to International Paper spraying 2,4,5-T near her home. The company insists that what it sprayed was not the since-banned 2,4,5-T but the presumably less toxic 2,4-D.

Another industry complaint is that all three documentaries were overloaded with interviews with emotional laymen with uneducated opinions, and that they employed scare tactics in showing rural residents of Oregon and Northern California with ugly skin rashes, birth defects, and other ailments they attributed to 2,4,5-T spraying. The documentary makers answer that emotionalism was justified.

"I don't see anything wrong with getting emotional about life and death matters that may affect you and your children," said Robert Richter, producer of "A Plague on Our Children." What's more, the deeply felt fear and anger of citizens who rightly or wrongly regard themselves as victims of chemical warfare are a legitimate part of the 2,4,5-T story.

Defenders of 2,4,5-T say all three documentaries exaggerated its toxicity. According to Dow Chemical, the herbicide contains only inconsequential amounts of the deadly dioxin that unavoidably contaminates it, and 2,4,5-T is no more toxic than aspirin or peanut butter. But many independent scientists disagree, and the Environmental Protection Agency was sufficiently alarmed by the high rate of miscarriages among women exposed to 2,4,5-T spraying that it suspended 2,4,5-T's use on forests and highway rights-of-way, while still permitting it on cattle grazing land and rice paddies.

Still another industry complaint is that the documentaries ignored the risks of alternatives to chemical spraying. Clearing brush and unwanted trees by hand instead of poisoning them from the sky would create many jobs while increasing the cost of producing lumber only slightly, according to government studies. But it would also lead to accidents from axes, chain saws, and falling trees, a point none of the documentaries made.

While all three documentaries stayed well within journalistic standards in taking the view that 2,4,5-T is a dangerous chemical the public should be protected against, KRON-TV went further. The San Francisco station followed its documentary with an editorial statement that said in part: "We hope 'Politics of Poison' makes you angry." It also drummed up 45,000 signatures petitioning Congress to investigate the EPA's long delay in banning the herbicide. And it rebroadcast the documentary on the eve of a referendum in Mendocino County that approved the nation's first ban on the aerial spraying of herbicides.

Dow Chemical has itself partly to blame for the public backlash against 2,4,5-T. Its zeal to defend the product has degenerated on occasion into self-defeating slurs on its critics. It has dismissed many 2,4,5-T opponents as illicit marijuana growers, put down ecologist Barry Commoner as a "publicity seeker," and alleged that "A Plague on Our Children" producer Robert Richter has "an obvious political bias."

Dow Chemical has also shown combativeness. When Dow public affairs manager Gary G. Jones wrote a letter of complaint following the airing of "A Plague on Our Children" and got back a reply he found unsatisfactory, Jones stamped producer Richter's reply "BULLSHIT" and mailed it back to him.

Johns-Manville is another defensive company that has harmed its own cause with invective. Its sweeping attacks have hit, among many targets, the 1979 recall of asbestos-lined hair dryers ("a media fraud aided and abetted by the Consumer Products Safety Commission") and media coverage of asbestos-related diseases ("deliberate distortion in the face of facts and out of a very apparent anti-business bias").

Industry has reacted defensively to even the most carefully documented and scrupulously balanced criticism. When the *National Geographic* published a 39-page article, "The Pesticide Dilemma," in February 1980, the National Agricultural Chemicals Association, representing pesticide manufacturers, attacked the article as "a one-sided perspective based on allegations and generalizations made without supporting references or data." However, the article reflected more than 200 interviews and 15 months' work for author Allen A. Boraiko, and was checked for accuracy before it was published with 50 government, medical, academic, and industry experts, including the head of the National Agricultural Chemicals Association. "The story held up under tremendous scrutiny," associate editor Joseph Judge said.

If the article had a weakness, it was slighting the economic trends that underlie agriculture's increasing use of pesticides. As American farms have evolved into capital-intensive, energy-hungry, mass-production businesses, many have minimized unit costs and maximized profits by specializing in only one or two crops. According to many experts, such monoculture greatly increases the need for pesticides and herbicides to fight the insects and weeds that thrive on the repetition of the same crop. Yet the *National Geographic* skipped over monoculture in a single sentence.

In addition to defensiveness, some companies have contributed to their bad press by not disclosing environmental hazards associated with their products. Take Xerox Corporation. When university researchers discovered a suspected cancer-causing impurity in the toner, or dry ink, used in many Xerox copying machines and reported their findings at a scientific conference, Xerox set to work with its toner supplier to reduce the impurity. But it didn't report the potential danger to either the government or the public.

The *Washington Star* broke the story in April 1980 and it soon spread across the country, alarming many Xerox machine operators. Xerox complained that some of the coverage distorted technical details and didn't mention the company's success in reducing the contaminant. But if Xerox had taken the initiative in disclosing the problem, rather than waiting for news of it to leak out, the coverage probably would have been more accurate and less damaging. By choosing silence in hopes of alarming nobody, Xerox ended up adding to the alarm.

Benefits of Media Warnings

Sometimes, of course, alarm is justified. The *Detroit News*'s series on cancer risks to General Motors wood model makers is a case in point. Despite GM's defensive reaction when the series started in November 1979, enough smoke emerged to indicate the likelihood of some fire. And enough action ensued to demonstrate the series' usefulness.

Besides angering GM, the series triggered three scientific studies—by the Michigan Cancer Foundation, the Memorial Sloan-Kettering Cancer Center of New York, and the National Institute of Occupational Safety and Health—that independently confirmed a significantly higher incidence of cancer among automobile model makers than in a comparable population group. The NIOSH study, in particular, confirmed a basis for the model makers' fears by determining that their greater susceptibility to cancer was probably caused by something in their work environment rather than by such personal factors as diet, socioeconomic status, or ethnic background.

No longer able to dismiss the cancer story as mostly rumor and gossip, General Motors inaugurated company-paid yearly physical exams and cancer detection tests for 4,000 employees in shops making models and patterns out of wood, plastic, and metal. It also took steps to reduce the wood and plastic dust, cutting oil mists and solvent vapors in its model shops. It didn't start requiring workers to wear the nose and mouth masks the company had long provided, but it set up a lunch-room outside the Fisher Body model shop and forbad workers to eat at their benches. Said a GM spokesman: "We still haven't anything to lead us to believe that the work environment is at fault, but we don't rule it out."

Meanwhile, the cancer inquiry spread to other GM plants, other auto manufacturers, and even other industries. Reports of a high incidence of lung cancer among workers at a GM body parts plant in Flint, Mich., prompted GM to review the way the plant handles four suspected carcinogenic materials, to offer employees lung X-rays, and to launch an antismoking campaign. In still another development, state authorities began looking into a reported high incidence of cancer among workers at a Goodyear Tire & Rubber Company plant in Jackson, Mich.

The *Detroit News* stayed on top of these and other developments as its close coverage of cancer and the workplace continued. A General Motors spokesman said the *News*'s continuing coverage was "straight-forward, fair and complete." But he remained critical of front-page headlines as over-blown and occasionally misleading. Several head-lines were indeed misleading. For instance, "CAN-CER TOLL UP FOR CAR TRADESMEN" on an early story implied that auto model makers were increasingly contracting cancer, whereas the paper had only learned of a few more individual cancer cases. And there's no question some front-page banner headlines were glaring. But these appeared only in early editions sold mostly on newsstands where big headlines are used to attract attention. The same stories carried smaller headlines in later editions that were mostly home-delivered.

Understandably, General Motors still wishes the *Detroit News* had privately alerted it to the model makers' fears and then waited before publishing anything until all the facts were in. "We don't need headlines to stir people up and send them scurrying about," GM chairman Murphy said. And just as understandably, the *Detroit News* chose to print the story piecemeal, as it developed, realizing that it might take years to assemble all the facts and even then they might prove inconclusive, and that meanwhile thousands of workers would continue to be exposed to possibly death-dealing substances. As editor William Giles explained in a column to readers: "The whole episode testifies to the need 'to stir people up.' Before the *News* stories appeared, the record shows, nobody in authority was stirred up. It seemed to some workers, in fact, that nobody even cared. . . . What the *News* reported— and properly—were the fears of the workers and the documentation showing the fears were not fantasy. If that 'stirred people up' to do something, even to pay attention, the newspaper accomplished a good bit. That's our business and the public's interest."

8

Puffery:
Free Publicity
for Business

Businessmen who complain about antibusiness bias
in the news media rarely acknowledge the pervasive
free publicity they manage to get into print and on
the air. Television allows representatives of the
food, clothing, home furnishings, and other industries to appear on interview talk shows and extol
the benefits of eating avocados, wearing the latest
ski fashions, redecorating the bathroom, and so
forth.

Radio has newscasters read commercials, which
can leave casual listeners thinking the commercials
are part of the news. Veteran ABC news commentator Paul Harvey, who delivers commercials in his
normally urgent and persuasive tone of voice, lends
his credibility as a journalist to the products he
endorses. Getting him to plug pork is "almost like
getting on the editorial page," the delighted National Pork Producers Council has said.

Magazines promote products in reader service
features. Women's magazines pepper their pages
with plugs for food, home furnishings, cosmetics,

and clothing. Hobby magazines enthuse over the latest in sporty cars, cameras, and camping equipment. Some city magazines favorably review restaurants that advertise, while ignoring those that do not.

A surprising number of metropolitan newspapers devote most of their real estate sections to publicizing condominium, townhouse, and subdivision developments, often at the expense of reporting on housing trends. Smaller dailies and weeklies publish business-supplied canned features that push just about everything from soup and nuts to microwave ovens and mobile homes.

Lowered Standards of Journalism

The businesses that originate such material argue that the public sees it for what it is, so no harm is done. But most journalists deplore unlabeled promotional material as inherently deceptive. Stories that imply an endorsement of a business and its products violate journalistic standards against editorializing in the news column. Puff pieces also compromise a newspaper's credibility and integrity, while shortchanging readers on reliable, disinterested information. As syndicated columnist Nicholas von Hoffman has noted: "The lowest standards of journalism, the greatest corruption, the most blatant pandering to advertisers goes on in the sections of the newspaper concerned with life's necessities as well as the subject areas that most personally engage us: food, real estate, fashion/clothing, cars, entertainment, sports, etc."

To be fair, many newspapers feel a responsibility to promote local business. Community newspapers often encourage readers to patronize local merchants. For instance, *The Ledger,* a Los Angeles suburban weekly, devoted a long article to a remodeled Thrifty Drug and Discount store with a "smashingly beautiful new look." The story enumerated the store's departments and range of merchandise, concluding that "shopping in the store will be so comfortable" that "everyone in Glendale will enjoy" doing so.

The *Los Angeles Herald Examiner* shifted its ad-poor real estate section from news department to advertising department control in 1978 to facilitate promotional coverage that the news department felt uncomfortable providing and to try to attract more ad linage. The *Herald Examiner* also offers advertisers unusual double exposure by publishing each week's real estate section twice—on Friday and again on Sunday.

More surprising is the willingness of advertising-plump metropolitan dailies to publish free publicity. One reason for this is that as prosperous papers have picked up advertising linage, they have had to increase the space devoted to news and features in order to keep their advertising-to-editorial ratio from becoming too lopsided. Faced with an increasing amount of space to fill, typically slim news staffs rely on filler and fluff supplied by business publicists to supplement their own coverage.

The *Los Angeles Times's* Sunday real estate section exemplifies the trend. The *Times's* real estate section has gained a nationwide reputation in recent years for extensive coverage of such industry developments as cut-rate brokerage commissions, home mortgage irregularities, vacation home time-sharing scams, and land planning disputes, and for printing readers' letters critical of building, lending,

and remodeling practices. However, the *Times*'s
real estate section is so fat with ads—50-page sections printed in two parts are common—that its
own staffers' stories can't provide all the copy
needed. So it takes up the slack with industry-
supplied news of personnel appointments, office
relocations, honors ("George J. Heltzer, a well-
known Southland builder, has been awarded the
Golden Trowel by the Southern California Plaster-
ing Institute") and other items of little or no interest to readers ouside the industry.

Like many papers, the *Times* also publishes commentary written by industry representatives. Ar-
mand L. Fontaine, an official of the American
Building Contractors Association, contributes a
weekly column, "Tips to Homeowners," that includes such self-serving advice as to hire licensed
contractors (whom Fontaine's group represents) in
preference to unlicensed home remodelers who
generally charge less but are harder to hold accountable. What with licensed contractors' business
"in a slow phase," Fontaine wrote one summer,
"now is an especially good time to talk to contractors . . . (A)ct today."

In addition to its Sunday real estate section,
which has been under news department control
since 1967, the *Los Angeles Times* has started a
series of Saturday real estate sections under advertising department control. Variously named "At
Home," "Carefree Living on the Westside," "Tri-
County Discoveries," and so forth, depending on
which circulation zone they are tailored for, the
Saturday real estate sections are labeled "classified
advertising supplement" on each page. The Saturday sections provide *Times* ad salesmen with the
powerful sales tool, "I can get a story in the paper

for you." The stories the salesmen promise—and deliver—are mostly advertiser-supplied publicity releases headlined and laid out to look like news stories. Promotional phrases abound: "serene location," "prestigious address," "carefree desert living," "panoramic views," "lushly landscaped grounds," "elegant," "opulent," "sophisticated," "secluded" and, of course, "moderately priced."

Newspapers that clearly identify advertising sections that have news formats are least likely to mislead readers and upset journalists. The *Los Angeles Herald Examiner* labels its real estate section "classified advertising." *The Register* of nearby Orange County tags its real estate section, "This is a *Register* advertising section." And the *St. Louis Post-Dispatch* alerts readers of both its Sunday real estate and automotive pages that "all material for this page [is] prepared by the advertising department." Many papers, however, use ambiguous phrases such as "classified display," and then only on inside pages.

Besides providing a vehicle for advertisers to reach prime prospects, real estate and other special-interest sections serve readers by providing basic information that helps them make purchasing decisions and cope with inflation. "Puffy articles on how to make this week's meat loaf may not be grand journalism, but they may be necessary to keep a newspaper's franchise," John Morton, newspaper stock analyst for John Muir & Company, has argued.

Special-interest sections can also be cash registers. Take food pages, which helped daily newspapers grab nearly $1 billion in food advertising in 1980. Food pages have burgeoned since the late

1940s when advertisers started vying for the income of families just beginning the baby boom.
The *Los Angeles Times's* Thursday food section
has grown so ad-fat that lately it has had to be
printed in two parts, while the *Chicago Tribune*
and several other dailies now publish food sections
twice a week.

Despite their considerable profitability, food
pages are generally produced on the cheap. Skimpy
budgets and skeletal staffs are the rule. Food editors, many with backgrounds in home economics
rather than journalism, often spend so much time
doing clerical chores—opening the mail, answering
cooking questions, filling requests for lost recipes—
that they have little time to edit copy, write headlines, and lay out pages, much less cover important
stories.

So to fill their pages most editors rely on publicity releases, photos, and recipes supplied by the
food industry. While food manufacturers plug individual brands, their trade associations push generic
categories—turkey, rice, mushrooms, sugar, and so
on. And the food editors pass the promotional
prose on to readers, exclamation points and all, as
in: "Beef and potatoes—what a winning combina-
tion! This tasty twosome complement each other
not only in appetite appeal, but in nutrition as
well." Although some papers attributed that filler
item to the National Live Stock and Meat Board,
most follow the practice of not telling readers
where industry-supplied photos and recipes come
from. Sometimes, though, the source is obvious, as
in a *Los Angeles Times* recipe for Roast Leg of
Pork with Pepsi-Cola.

Few newspapers have the time, staff, and kit-
chen to test recipes before publishing them. And

thousands of small dailies and weeklies neither edit nor set type for the canned recipes they use. Indeed, inserting ready-to-print canned copy in the paper is so effortless that papers easily lose track of what they've printed. The *San Marcos Outlook,* a San Diego County weekly that devotes most of its second page to canned features, has been known to print canned recipes twice. "If they send us two sets of releases, and we don't throw one away, we pick it up inadvertently," Editor William Carroll explained.

Newspapers that print their food pages in color can save hundreds of dollars per page in photography and preprinting costs by using entire canned color food pages. Sun Color Service, a major supplier, sends out 70 to 80 canned color food pages each year and each page is used by an average of 180 newspapers. "We're a bonanza for smaller papers whose food editors can't develop their own material," according to Dorothy Rabb, manager of the firm's Colormat division.

Typically, a canned color page contains a large photo of an elaborate meal, an article, and half a dozen recipes. Some companies, among them Pillsbury Company, pay Sun Color Service to produce and distribute a page plugging just its brands. But it's more common for two to four companies and trade associations to cosponsor a page. A 1980 page headlined "BEAUTIFUL, BOUNTIFUL BRUNCH" was sponsored by the National Turkey Federation, the Cling Peach Advisory Board, and the American Home Foods division of American Home Products Corporation. The sponsors' names didn't appear on the page, but the ingredients called for in the recipes included turkey, peaches, and such American Home Foods brands as Chef-Boy-ar-dee Beefogetti, Gulden's mustard, and Zippy avocado filling.

While food sections keep busy promoting food, entertainment sections give fulsome and generally enthusiastic coverage to new movies and television specials. And sports sections do the same with local teams, while blowing some national sports events out of proportion.

No athletic contest is as heavily covered as the National Football League's championship game. Christened the Super Bowl by sports writers, this annual event rivals the major political conventions as spectacle and extravaganza. More than 1,200 reporters, editors, photographers, and broadcasters covered the 1980 Super Bowl in Pasadena. The National Football League happily facilitated coverage of the 1980 Super Bowl by providing favored journalists with the use of Buicks for several days before the game to get from their hotels to team practices, press conferences, and parties. And on the day of the game the NFL assigned 20 public relations men to locker rooms to gather quotes from coaches and players for deadline-harried writers in the press box.

The *Oakland Tribune*'s morning edition, *Eastbay Today*, devoted the equivalent of two and a half pages a day to the 1980 Super Bowl during the week before the game. However, "the enormous publicity buildup that always precedes the contest creates expectations that are difficult to fulfill," *The Wall Street Journal*'s sports columnist, Frederick C. Klein, has complained. "As far as many fans are concerned, a better name for the event might be the Stupor Bowl."

To be fair, many newspaper sports sections try to hold commercialism to a minimum. But this is becoming increasingly difficult with the proliferation of sports events sponsored by businesses to promote their names and products. Typical of these events are the Pizza Hut Classic College Basketball Game, the Jack-in-the-Box Invitational Track Meet, and the Lady Michelob Golf Tournament.

Sports sponsors drum up coverage by inviting reporters and sometimes their wives on expense-paid trips to distant golf tournaments and other events. Some papers permit writers to accept such junkets, but an increasing number do not. According to *Los Angeles Times* sports editor Bill Shirley, "You have to avoid the appearance of being in their pocket, and the best way to do that is to pay your own way." The "we'll pay our own way" trend has cut down on the number of junkets that journalists used to count on as a fringe benefit of their job. For instance, the Big Three domestic auto manufacturers have stopped paying the expenses of auto writers attending their press preview showings of new models, although several foreign manufacturers still do.

Old-fashioned press agentry is far from passé, however. Food manufacturers still stage cooking contests and other "newsworthy" events and pay food editors' way to them. And Hollywood still runs junkets to hype new movies. For instance, 70 writers were flown to Arizona in 1979 to attend the world premier of *Meteor,* interview the movie's stars, and explore such scenic wonders as the bottom of a 570-foot meteor crater where bartenders in white ties and tails served them Meteor beer flown in from France. Only one fourth of the journalists paid their own way.

Airlines, hotel chains and foreign governments vie for the attention of travel writers with expense-paid trip offers. Many papers that forbid their own staff writers to accept such trips nonetheless publish travel articles by freelance writers who can't afford to pay their own way to distant places. After accepting a free plane ride or room and meals, a freelance writer understandably finds it difficult to criticize an airline or hotel.

Uncritical travel section articles on far-off places do armchair travelers no harm. But food, real estate, auto, and other sections that deal with life's necessities do their readers a disservice when they allow promotional coverage to crowd out basic, reliable information. Realizing this, some food sections have begun supplementing the customary recipes and human interest stories about food with articles on controversies—for instance, the safety of food additives and the appropriateness of electronic grocery checkout systems. Some are probing what goes into food products, as the *Washington Post* did for several years with its "Label of the Week" feature, which listed the ingredients of a food product and asked readers to guess the brand. The listing usually revealed a long string of chemical ingredients and sometimes the absence of the presumed main ingredient—chocolate in chocolate chip cookies, for instance.

The *Milwaukee Journal*, whose food section is among the most independent of the food industry, occasionally critiques food products. A critique of pet foods found some "a little deceiving. Ken-L-Ration Special Cuts, for instance, have the appearance of beefy stew meat," but contain "more chicken parts, corn syrup, cornstarch and water than anything else."

**Some
Newspapers
Avoid
Controversy**

Still, most food sections continue to steer clear of controversy. Take what happened at the *Washington Star* when consumer columnist Goody Solomon submitted a five-part series on cents-off grocery coupons. The well-researched series gave a balanced view of the controversy surrounding couponing, quoting both promoters and critics. It pointed out that coupons slow down supermarket checkout lines and suggested that shoppers might "benefit more by across-the-board price reductions instead of coupon offers." After running the first article under the headline, "COUPONING: WHO GETS CLIPPED?" the *Washington Star* abruptly and without explanation killed the remaining four articles.

Real estate sections also are less helpful to readers than they could be. Few point out inferior materials and construction defects in new houses. The quality of life in new residential communities gets little attention. And help to readers on cutting the cost of buying and selling homes is rare. Some newspapers black out real estate brokers who offer cut-rate commissions. And the *Burbank* (Calif.) *Daily Review* fired a women's page editor for giving the author of *How to Sell (and Buy) Your Home Without a Broker* a favorable write-up.

Travel sections similarly keep coverage noncontroversial, even when this means overlooking perils confronting tourists. However, as the list of places around the world to be avoided because of repression, violence, and crime grows, travel sections that ignore unpleasantries risk sending their readers off on misguided tours.

The *New York Times's* travel section was among the first to warn of rising violent crime against

tourists in Hawaii. But then the section ran a
lengthy article in 1980 encouraging travel to South
Korea, assuring readers that "with the country
moving toward democratic reform, the mood of
the capital (Seoul) has become much more exuber-
ant." Readers of that Sunday's *New York Times*
must have blinked when they reached that upbeat
story in the travel section, after being informed on
the front page of the *Times*'s main news section
that 300 riot policemen in Seoul had just broken
up a gathering of university student leaders seeking
democratic reforms. The lead story began: "Faced
with the most serious student political unrest in 20
years, the South Korean Government announced
this morning that it was closing the universities,
prohibiting political gatherings and labor strikes,
imposing rigorous press censorship, and extending
martial law to the entire country."

The *Los Angeles Times* was similarly caught in
1980 in an embarrassing discrepancy between the
world of reality reported in its news sections and
the world of romance portrayed in a Sunday feature section. Several weeks after publishing news of
desperate Haitians fleeing poverty and hunger in
unseaworthy boats, the paper's "Home" magazine
section rhapsodized about "the intoxicating charms
and mysteries of Haiti," its "whimsical" ginger-
bread architecture, "colorful folksy" art, "charm-
ing Creole tongue," and the natives' "friendly so-
ciable manner." Grinding poverty and the repressive
regime of President Jean-Claude Duvalier weren't
even hinted at. By coincidence, that same Sunday's
travel section also had an upbeat story on Haiti
("without a doubt the safest tourist destination in
the entire Caribbean—as well as the friendliest").
But at least it contained a passing reference to
poverty and hunger—inserted at the last minute on

instructions from top *Times* editors. However, the "Home" section had already been printed and its Haiti coverage couldn't be altered.

Although the publication of promotional material is almost always good for the businesses supplying it, it isn't always good for a newspaper's own business. When the *Los Angeles Times* devoted the front page of its Sunday real estate section to three or four illustrated articles featuring new housing projects, which it stopped doing in 1976, readers regarded the stories as endorsements and rushed by the hundreds to the openings. Recalled real estate editor Dick Turpin: "It was great publicity for the builder—so good he didn't need an ad."

And when it comes to selling ideas rather than houses, businessmen still don't need an ad to get their viewpoints across in the media. The increasing number of businesses using newspapers and television to disseminate corporate advocacy can attest to that.

9

Advocacy: Getting
Business Views
Across

Television newsman Martin Agronsky, anchoring a "special report" on the fertilizer industry, announces, "We take you now to Donaldsonville, La., and Joan Levetter."

Joan Levetter, standing in front of a plant that makes ammonia, a component of chemical fertilizer, interviews a plant official, then sums up: "If we didn't supplement our soil with nitrogen-bearing compounds, millions of the world's cupboards would be bare, and food prices would skyrocket. Fertilization is not merely desirable; it is essential. This is Joan Levetter reporting. Martin?"

Back in the studio, Martin Agronsky looks at what appears to be a TV monitor on which he presumably can see correspondent Levetter, says, "Thank you, Joan," and continues his narration.

Just another dull television news feature? So it must have seemed to TV viewers in San Francisco, New Orleans, Cincinnati, and other cities. But "And One to Grow On" was no ordinary TV news feature. For one thing, it was produced not by any news organization but by the chemical fertilizer industry. For another, the newsroom, anchor desk, and TV monitor were all fake. Agronsky only pretended to be able to see and talk with reporters in the field. And they weren't reporters. "Joan Levetter," for one, is actually an actress under another name.

The Fertilizer Institute, which is the trade association of manufacturers of chemical fertilizers, said it made "And One to Grow On" to help disassociate fertilizers in the public's mind from the unfavorable publicity that has tarnished pesticides. It said it chose a television newscast format to give the 18-minute film immediacy and credibility, and it omitted any reference to the Fertilizer Institute's sponsorship to enhance the film's acceptance by TV as a "public service" program.

Agronsky, a former correspondent for each of the three TV networks who went on to moderate the nationally distributed panel-discussion show "Agronsky and Company," said he didn't realize when he made the film in 1979 that it would be shown on television. "I wouldn't have jeopardized my career if I had regarded this in any sense as impinging on my work as a journalist, or the public's perception of me as a journalist."

It was, however, Agronsky's journalistic credentials rather than his acting skills that landed him the anchorman part. "An actor doesn't have the authority or credibility that a newsman has," a Fertilizer Institute spokesman explained. "The public presumes actors can be paid to say anything, whereas newsmen say what they believe to be the facts."

**Manifold
Tactics: Some
Aboveboard . . .**

Hiring newsmen to lend authority and credibility to industry's version of the facts is only one of many weapons business is wielding nowadays to influence public opinion and government legislation and regulation. Standing up and sounding off on public issues marks a turning point in corporate communications strategy that many businessmen and even some business critics consider long overdue. Much of this effort is entirely aboveboard and improving impressively in quality. Corporations and trade associations are producing radio and TV programs that are clearly identified as theirs. They are taking properly labeled advertisements in newspapers and on the air to present their positions, answer their critics, and improve business's public image. A few are even taking pains to include opposing views along with their own.

The new drive to speak out, however, is also bringing with it some practices that tend to blur the distinction between factual reporting and advocacy. Business is supplying prerecorded interviews with business advocates to television and radio stations, which slip them into newscasts, usually without reference to their source. And business is flooding small newspapers with ready-to-use canned editorials, columns, and cartoons that carry hidden corporate messages. The radio and television stations and newspapers that use canned material without identifying its source share responsibility for misleading the public into assuming the material is objective journalism rather than one-sided business advocacy.

These practices infuriate some public-interest groups and other critics who wish business would get back in the corporate closet. The critics consider much business advocacy plain propaganda—

some call it "corporatprop"—and they complain it is overwhelming the media with a single viewpoint. Rhoda H. Karpatkin, executive director of Consumers Union, has gone so far as to contend that the "colossal imbalance" of business advocacy "poses a threat to political democracy as we know it."

As Karpatkin notes, business's stepped-up use of the media is only the most visible aspect of a far-reaching business blitz. Corporations are also showering schools with free films, pamphlets, and lesson plans that teach economics from the corporate point of view. At universities, corporations are endowing professorships of free enterprise, funding executive-in-residence programs, and subsidizing Students in Free Enterprise clubs. They are pumping money into university research projects and conservative think tanks—and getting studies that provide ideological ammunition in return. They are generating letters from their employees and others to influence congressional legislation. And they are setting up public affairs offices in Washington and moving industry trade associations there to lobby for favorable legislation and to gain access to the large Washington press corps.

No group better exemplifies the aboveboard portion of business's advocacy offensive than the U.S. Chamber of Commerce. Not content to depend on traditional dissemination of information and policy statements to the news media, the Chamber has created its own media programs to take business's message directly into American homes. Besides publishing *Nation's Business,* whose 1.3 million circulation makes it the most widely distributed business magazine, the Chamber in 1979 started a weekly newspaper, *Washington Report,* that it soon was sending to 750,000 subscribers. And to supplement the weekly panel discussion program, "What's the Issue?" that it has distributed free to 400 radio stations for years, the Chamber began in 1979 to produce a weekly television panel discussion show, "It's Your Business."

Rather than presenting just business's side, "It's Your Business" fosters lively debate between liberal congressmen, labor union leaders, consumer advocates, and others on one side, and conservative congressmen, corporate executives, and other business advocates on the other side. Of the four panelists on each program, one appears every week—Richard Lesher, the Chamber's president. "It's Your Business," which was carried by 128 commercial TV stations by the end of 1980, is eventually to be produced in the Chamber's own $4 million studios at its headquarters in downtown Washington. The studios are to have the capacity to beam this and other programs by satellite direct to TV stations and cable TV systems across the country. Other programs on business and economics that the Chamber foresees telecasting include a half-hour weekly business news program, educational programs for high school students, and occasional prime-time specials.

...and Some Questionable

Corporations are also innovating in disseminating advocacy. Consider Mobil Corporation. With a public relations staff of 73 and a public relations budget of $21 million in 1980, Mobil is among corporate America's most active and visible advocates. Well known for its sponsorship of quality television drama and its newspaper opinion ads, Mobil is also getting its message out in less obvious ways, including feeding "special reports" and interviews to television.

Since 1976, Mobil has produced at least a dozen televised special reports on such energy issues as oil exploration, gasoline prices, and government policy. Each half-hour report features a TV journalist interviewing Mobil executives and other experts who support the company's energy positions. Mobil sends the special reports free to television stations, which typically air them late at night and on weekends. The reports acknowledge Mobil's involvement only in a credit line that flashes briefly on the screen at the end: "Produced for Mobil Oil by DWJ Associates."

Sixty-two stations have shown "Energy at the Crossroads," a 1980 Mobil special report that is typical of the genre. "Energy at the Crossroads" features reporter Roger Sharp interviewing Mobil Vice President Bonner Templeton, former Department of Energy Deputy Secretary John O'Leary, Virginia Governor John Dalton, and others. Templeton argues for more government incentives for oil exploration, as well as "some environmental trade-offs." O'Leary assures viewers that the energy shortage is "not a product of oil company manipulation" but rather the fault of federal policymakers and an overconsuming public. Governor Dalton calls for the government to ease restrictions on nuclear, coal, and oil development. "Energy at the Crossroads" also shows economist Arthur Laffer of the University of Southern California telling students that government energy regulations and taxes are excessive. And at Opinion Research Corporation, pollster Kenneth Schwartz discusses a survey in which 52 percent of those polled agreed that the cost of government regulation outweighs the benefits.

"Energy at the Crossroads" is as notable for what it leaves out as for what it includes. For one thing, there is no hint that the seemingly neutral interviews were conducted by a Mobil retainer. For another, there were no interviews with environmentalists or others whose views would have balanced the energy-exploitation advocacy of those interviewed.

Roger Sharp, a political reporter for WABC-TV in New York when not free-lancing for Mobil and other corporations, is among half a dozen reporters who have placed their credibility as objective journalists in Mobil's service. Others include Mort Crim, anchorman at WDIV-TV in Detroit; Marcia Rose, a free-lance and former anchorwoman at KYW-TV in Philadelphia; and C. P. Gilmore, a free-lance science reporter for WNEW-TV in New York under the name of Ken Gilmore, as well as full-time editor of *Popular Science* magazine.

All four of these journalists have defended their role as Mobil interviewers. Mobil may have selected the experts to be interviewed, they said, but it imposed no restrictions on the questions asked. The journalists maintained their role as interviewer didn't constitute an endorsement of the views expressed by those interviewed. What's more, Mobil had no obligation to include interviews with critics of its energy policies. In short, said Roger Sharp, "It was honest corporate flackery."

Slickly produced corporate flackery such as Mobil's finds a ready outlet at hundreds of television stations with skimpy budgets for producing news and public service programming of their own. Stations that have expanded their local newscasts in recent years are especially eager for business-supplied free footage that helps fill air time and holds down costs.

Mobil has assisted stations with slack time during newscasts by breaking up each of its half-hour special reports into individual interviews and sending these out to be inserted in local newscasts. Mobil estimated that 110 stations slipped individual interviews from its half-hour "Energy at the Crossroads" into their newscasts, typically without identifying Mobil as the source. "In most cases, viewers get the impression that the interview is the station's own," Anthony J. DeNigro, manager of media programs for Mobil, said. "We make certain that everything we send out is identified. But what stations decide to do then is their business."

Although Mobil prefers to use journalists as interviewers, other business advocates cast public relations agents and actors in that role. The Sugar Association used its New York publicist to interview association President J. W. Tatem, Jr., for a "Spot News Service special report" that some 65 radio stations aired. The publicist, identified only as Dick Cunningham, asked questions that enabled Tatem to defend sugary foods against proposed federal restrictions on TV advertising to children. "The presweetened cereals have less sugar in them than what a person normally adds to the cereal when they want sugar," Tatem said. "The food industry really is just carrying on what grandmother used to do at home."

Suzanne Leamer, an actress in television commercials and former Miss California beauty queen, interviews business advocates for a talk show called "Viewpoint" that by the end of 1980 was beamed to 415 cable TV systems connected to 3 million homes. A corporation or trade association that wants to tell its message quickly in a believable, informal format, and with the assurance that only friendly questions will be asked, provides Leamer in advance of the interview with a list of questions. And then she asks them.

Business spokesmen she interviewed on "Viewpoint" in 1980 included a Ford Motor Company lobbyist who predicted that fuel-efficient American cars would soon substantially reduce foreign autos' penetration of the U.S. market, a representative from Campbell Soup Company's Swanson Frozen Food division who promoted microwave cooking as safe and energy-efficient, and a Dow Chemical Company official who argued that the chemical industry, far from deserving blame for causing cancer, was responsible for only about 1 percent of cancers. Even Dow production workers "are safer at work than they are at home," he said.

Modern Satellite Network, which produces "Viewpoint," has charged businesses $6,000 for each five-minute interview. The fee includes transmitting the interview on six different days to the 415 cable systems that receive Modern Satellite Network programming. The network is operated by Modern Talking Picture Service, a leading distributor of business films to schools, community groups, and TV.

The business films that Modern distributes to both over-the-air and cable TV range widely in style and sophistication. Some are crude propaganda. For instance, a Dow Chemical film, "Man's

Material Welfare," defends capitalism by asking such questions as, "Which do you want—slave or free, socialism or free enterprise?" In contrast, the California Redwood Association, a lumber industry group, uses a soft-sell approach in "In Search of the Last Redwood" to reassure the public that despite extensive clear-cutting, the giant trees are so plentiful that "you can't wipe them out."

Business advocacy intended for inclusion in local TV news programs similarly varies. When Pan American World Airways was seeking government approval of its acquisition of National Airlines in 1979, it used a canned feature service to prepare and send out several sets of color slides to be shown on the air, accompanied by scripts to be read by local newscasters. Not only were the scripts not attributed to Pan Am, but some made debatable claims. For instance, one script asserted that the Pan Am acquisition of National Airlines "could lead to a better balance of trade and slow the inflation rate." Pan Am defended the statement about improving the U.S. balance of trade as "reasonable," saying it expected the takeover to enable it to compete more effectively against foreign airlines for fares to and within the United States. But Pan Am conceded the statement about slowing the inflation rate was "stretching it a bit."

Atlantic Richfield Company's approach to television has been far more credible—and costly. In 1979 Arco began producing monthly "Energy Update" programs. Each half-hour program consisted of three energy-related stories. Some stories didn't mention Arco, and others included comment from oil industry critics. Anthony P. Hatch, Arco's manager of media relations and producer and host of "Energy Update," said at least two dozen TV stations aired all or part of the program in its first year. However, when a station inserted a segment from "Energy Update" in a local newscast, there was no guarantee it properly identified the source as Arco, and Hatch said, "we don't care if Arco isn't given credit."

The Corporate Legionnaires

Corporations eager to get their story told are sending out spokesmen as well as videotaped releases. Oil industry executives became particularly active on panel interview shows such as "Meet the Press," "Face the Nation," and "Issues and Answers" after the 1979 fuel shortage and price run-up. John Swearingen, the blunt, occasionally brusque chairman of Standard Oil Company (Ind.), appeared on more than a dozen network and nationally syndicated shows to defend the oil industry, criticize "punitive" taxation, and urge gasoline conservation.

Some companies conduct local talk show blitzes. To help beat back congressional moves to break up the giant oil companies, Mobil once sent 21 executives to 21 cities where in a couple of days they appeared on more than a hundred talk shows, news broadcasts and radio call-in programs. It's more common, though, for a single company representative to stump the talk show circuit. For instance, Shell Chemical Company dispatched toxicologist Kathy Sommer on a week-long tour to six television and nine radio stations (plus two newspapers) to spread the word that there was no occupational cancer epidemic and no need for more stringent federal standards to protect workers from carcinogens.

Industry associations often retain academicians as consultants and pay their expenses to appear on talk shows. The National Agricultural Chemicals

Association has booked William A. Harvey, a retired University of California at Davis weed-control expert, on many talk show tours. On a typical stop, at WEWS-TV in Cleveland, Harvey defended pesticides as vital "to help starving nations of the world with their food supply." Typically, the station failed to identify him as a spokesman for a group representing pesticide manufacturers.

Although local talk show interviewers usually ask only friendly questions, shows with studio or call-in audiences pose the ever-present hazard of hostile questions. When Swearingen of Standard Oil appeared on Phil Donahue's nationally distributed TV interview show, a woman in the audience asked how Swearingen could preach gasoline conservation when he himself rode around in a gas-guzzling Lincoln.

Although Swearingen had trouble answering that one, business generally has become more adept, as well as more active, in responding to criticism. Mobil, for one, has made a practice of taping replies to radio and television station editorials that annoy it. Stations that have editorialized in support of special state sales taxes on oil companies have received—and aired—replies taped by Mobil accusing the stations of exhibiting "an antibusiness, anti-oil bias" and using their "special broadcast powers to urge select punitive taxes on the oil industry and ultimately on the consumer."

Full-fledged rebuttals to criticism of business have also been cropping up. When CBS's "60 Minutes" charged Illinois Power Company in 1979 with mismanaging the construction of a nuclear power plant, causing delays and huge cost overruns, the company not only got "60 Minutes" to

correct two major errors on the air, but it also produced a video rebuttal. The 42-minute rebuttal,
"60 Minutes: Our Reply," included the entire 16-
minute "60 Minutes" segment interspersed with
additional footage and comment expanding on
areas that the company contended CBS "edited
out, presented incorrectly, or chose to ignore."
Among other things, the rebuttal effectively chal-
lenged the credibility of two employees whom Illinois Power had fired for unsatisfactory work and
who subsequently were interviewed on "60 Minutes." Illinois Power distributed more than 2,000
copies of "60 Minutes: Our Reply" for showings
by corporations, trade associations, journalism
schools, and community organizations. Some members of Congress and their staffs also saw it, and its
status as an instant classic was confirmed when
"CBS News Sunday Morning" commented on the
film and showed two brief excerpts from it.

Another video rebuttal, the one-hour "Uranium:
Fact or Fiction?" was aired in its entirety on two
TV stations. "Uranium: Fact or Fiction?" rebutted
an ABC documentary, "The Uranium Factor," that
portrayed the uranium industry as well as federal
and New Mexico authorities, as lax in protecting
uranium miners, mill workers, and the environment
from radiation and other hazards. The rebuttal was
produced by uranium industry supporters at
KOAT-TV in Albuquerque, N.M., near the heart of
the uranium mining industry. KOAT aired it and so
did KJCT-TV in Grand Junction, Colo.

Robert Goralski, an NBC White House correspondent who went on to become Washington information director for Gulf Oil Company, hosted
the rebuttal and conducted some of the interviews
shown on it. One person Goralski interviewed was

a training coordinator at a big Gulf Oil uranium mine ("Joe, tell me about the safety training program here at Mt. Taylor..."). However, nowhere in the rebuttal was Goralski identified as a Gulf Oil employee himself, leaving "Uranium: Fact or Fiction?" as vulnerable to criticism as "The Uranium Factor" it was criticizing.

Although there never was any chance ABC would give up 60 minutes of air time to broadcast "Uranium: Fact or Fiction?" the network did agree to air an unedited 4-minute rebuttal by another complainant, Kaiser Aluminum & Chemical Corporation. The Kaiser rebuttal, defending the company against a 1980 report by "20/20" that Kaiser had knowingly marketed unsafe aluminum house wiring, was to have been inserted in a subsequent episode of "20/20." But after agreeing to that forum, ABC changed its mind and insisted the rebuttal air instead on its "Nightline" news program. Kaiser accused ABC of reneging and filed a $40 million slander suit against the network. Meanwhile, its videotaped rebuttal remained in the can.

Like Kaiser, a growing number of businesses are insisting on maximum control over what they say and when they say it. And to tell their story exactly the way they want it told, without editing by journalists presumed to have liberal biases, more and more corporations and trade associations are turning to paid advertising.

Advocacy ads that present business's perspective on public issues are nothing new, of course. Warner & Swasey Company, the Cleveland machine tool manufacturer, has run more than 1,100 ads since 1939 promoting private enterprise, defending profits, criticizing government regulation, deficit spending, and aid to foreign countries, and taking stands on other issues. But advocacy advertising has burgeoned in recent years as business, confronted by growing public distrust and stiffening government regulation, has begun to answer its critics and present its case more forcefully. The nuclear industry has mounted large advertising campaigns to argue that nuclear power is safe and essential and to help defeat antinuclear referenda. The oil industry has taken ads to defend soaring prices and profits. And the chemical industry has used ads to counter public perceptions that it is contaminating the country with toxic pollutants and needs to be reined in by Washington.

Industry has generally encountered no difficulty placing its advocacy ads in newspapers and magazines. But the television networks traditionally have rejected nearly all advocacy ads, contending that complex, controversial issues cannot be dealt with adequately in 60-second commercials. The networks also fear public-issue commercials would bore or antagonize some viewers, while possibly obligating the networks under the Fairness Doctrine to provide free time for opposing viewpoints.

Effectiveness of Advocacy Ads

Cracks began appearing in the networks' wall against advocacy advertising in 1980 when ABC and NBC accepted Kaiser Aluminum commercials expressing mild views on energy, youth employment, and voting. Then ABC announced a one-year limited experiment with advocacy ads, saying that starting in July 1981 it would accept one such ad each night, but only for airing after midnight.

Individual TV stations are considerably less standoffish than the networks. A 1980 poll of

nearly 400 TV stations found 89 percent willing
to accept advocacy ads, up from 50 percent in a
similar survey five years earlier. Forty-three stations showed a 1980 series of Mobil commercials
expressing strong views on energy policy, taxation,
government regulation, and other issues, and no
station turned them down. The commercials featured an anchorman-like authority at "Mobil Information Center" and reporter-like commentators in
the field urging government policies to step up
domestic energy development.

Are advocacy ad campaigns effective? Some
clearly seem to be. For instance, a W. R. Grace &
Company 1978 ad campaign arguing for a reduction in capital gains taxes is credited by some experts as having helped influence Congress to reduce
the capital gains tax rate. And Kaiser Aluminum's
full-page ads in 10 newspapers alleging that the
"20/20" report on unsafe aluminum wiring constituted "trial by television" may have contributed to
ABC's initial decision to put Kaiser's unedited
rebuttal on the air. On the other hand, ad campaigns that carry obviously one-sided and self-
serving messages probably turn off as many readers
and viewers as they persuade.

While many businesses step up advocacy advertising in hopes of winning allies, some businesses
are withholding advertising as a way to punish journalists. For instance, Honeywell, Inc., withdrew
some $500,000 in advertising from *Business Week*
over an unfavorable 1978 article on the company's
computer operations and didn't resume advertising
until 1980. Johns-Manville Corporation pulled
$150,000 in ads from *Fortune* in 1978 over an
article on a management shakeup and was still out
of all Time Inc. magazines two years later. On the

local level, all nine new car dealers in Salina, Kan., boycotted the *Salina Journal* for six weeks in 1980 to protest the newspaper's editorial endorsement of a 0.5 percent city sales tax. The boycott ended when the tax was defeated in a referendum.

Journalists generally deplore such advertiser retaliation as overreactive and ineffective. But conservative newspaper columnist Patrick Buchanan thinks a little intimidation is good for the media. He has said that what "these puppies of the press need (is) to be given an occasional jerk on the leash of the advertising dollar."

Using rather than abusing the media remains the key to corporate advocacy efforts, however. And one of the cheapest uses of the media to create an environment favorable to business interests is the public service announcement. Public service announcements are the noncommercial messages that newspapers and magazines publish without charge and that radio and television stations and networks squeeze between programs and commercials. PSAs are supposed to perform a public service by giving people vital information. They are not supposed to promote commercial interests or be politically partisan.

Despite these strictures, many PSAs are thinly disguised corporate propaganda. Take the slick 60-second PSA "presented as a public service by Mobil Corporation" that 185 TV stations aired. Showing a small boy and girl on a nature hunt, the PSA warns: "Today, the research efforts of U.S. industry are actually lagging because of costly government regulations and discouraging taxation.... So let's not hobble American research with regulations and taxation that stifle creative minds. Let's give

Tommy and Sue and anybody else the chance they
deserve to make America a better place to live."

The Advertising Council, a corporate-funded
group that produces public service advertising campaigns, shares Mobil's abhorrence of government
regulation. The Ad Council thinks its public service
campaign on the American economic system has
helped turn public opinion against regulation.
Since the campaign started in 1976, the proportion
of Americans who think there is too much government regulation rose from 42 percent of those
polled at the Council's initiative to 60 percent in
1980.

"You Are the American Economic System," a
32-page booklet the Advertising Council published
and distributed as part of this campaign, seeks to
convince the ordinary citizen that his or her influence, not government regulators', is decisive.
Among the booklet's simplistic statements: "As a
voter you regulate what you produce and the way
you produce." "You determine utility rates." "You
govern controls on pesticides." "You govern advertising claims."

Long evident in public service advertising, business advocacy is also becoming significant in public
television. This hasn't always been so. Corporations
have traditionally concentrated their contributions
to public TV on quality drama, science documentaries, and other noncontroversial programs that
appeal to educated audiences and help position the
corporations as generous benefactors of culture.
Corporations have generally avoided funding investigative documentaries and other public affairs programming. Even "Consumer Survival Kit," an upbeat weekly program that gave consumers informa-

tion without pointing the finger at business, never could secure national corporate underwriting and went off the air after five seasons on PBS.

Business Advocacy on Public TV

As corporations take a more active role in explaining their activities and defending their positions, they have started to put money into public TV programs that espouse business causes. For example, corporations provided substantial funding for conservative commentator William F. Buckley, Jr.'s "Firing Line" talk show in 1980 for the first time since it began on PBS in 1971.

Corporations and corporate foundations were so taken with economist Milton Friedman's libertarian, monetarist proposals, which include scrapping the welfare system and most government regulation, that they funded his 10-part series, "Free to Choose." They also underwrote two series by Ben J. Wattenberg, a senior fellow at the conservative American Enterprise Institute for Public Policy Research and a self-professed "great advocate of the free enterprise system."

Wattenberg's first series, the 13-part "In Search of the Real America" in 1977-78, included a segment, "There's No Business Like Big Business," that argued that most corporations, far from being greedy and insensitive, are responsive to the needs of consumers and society. The second series, "Ben Wattenberg's 1980," argued that the government has gone far enough in taxing and regulating the private economy.

Not surprisingly, business is a lot freer with funds for public TV programs that espouse its causes than for nonideological programs that

merely explain how business works. Public TV
station WGBH in Boston not only encountered
difficulty lining up corporate underwriting for a
13-part series on business called "Enterprise" that
it planned to put on PBS in the fall of 1981, but it
also encountered resistance to its reporting efforts.
Even though the series' producers worked in con-
junction with the Harvard Business School, they
reported finding it "awfully tough to get a corporation, particularly a large one, to agree to let even
well-meaning, well-versed, well-connected video
journalists such as ourselves inside." Some two
dozen corporations declined cooperation, according to "Enterprise" executive editor Paul Solman.

Another projected series, "Made in U.S.A.," has
run up against what critics of public television
complain is a double standard. Although it accepts
financing from corporations for programs about
business, PBS initially rejected any labor union
funding for the 10-part "Made in U.S.A." series on
American labor history. Under fire, PBS subsequently set a limit of one-third union funding, tac-
itly drawing back from its presumption that unions
have a direct self-interest in a series on labor history, whereas corporations have no direct self-
interest in business-oriented series such as Friedman's and Wattenberg's.

**Blanketing
the Media**

Although television's huge audiences and its
visual impact make it a prize target for business
advocates, the advocates aren't neglecting any medium, even small newspapers. Each small-town or
suburban daily or weekly may reach only several
thousand readers, but the total circulation of the
3,000 to 4,000 such papers served by canned feature services runs into the millions.

For a fee, canned feature services write, illus-
trate, print up, and distribute corporate messages
in the form of columns, cartoons, and other features. Newspapers receive this material at no charge
and publish it without having to set type. Besides
cutting a newspaper's costs, ready-to-use canned
material is often more sprightly written and more
brightly illustrated than the paper could afford on
its own.

A touch of humor is often used to ease down a
lump of propaganda. To fight mandatory air bag
regulations, Chrysler Corporation distributed a cartoon depicting a motorist engulfed in an air bag
that accidentally inflated when his car's hood was
closed. The connection to Chrysler wasn't stated.

To fight environmental restrictions, Mobil used a
canned cartoon showing two divers swimming
under an offshore oil drilling platform and being
menaced by two huge sharks. Said one shark to the
other: "Forget it, Charlie—those oil-exploration
people are almost on the 'endangered species' list!"
Mobil's cartoons, which have been distributed by
Associated Release Service, Inc., of Chicago, have
all carried an accompanying disclaimer, "Note to
editors: Brought to you by Mobil Corporation."
But the cartoons themselves haven't mentioned
Mobil, so readers have been unaware of their origin.

Critics object that cartoons that pose as entertainment but actually carry a corporate message
are sneaky. But Ronald N. Levy, president of North
American Precis Syndicate, Inc., a canned service
based in New York, defends unlabeled corporate
advocacy. "The public doesn't know where most of
the material in newspapers comes from," he said.
"It still doesn't know who Deep Throat was. The

validity of news isn't determined by the source, but by its accuracy and news value."

Critics also object to editorials that appear to be the considered, independent product of local editors but actually are self-serving industry advocacy disseminated from afar. The AFL-CIO contends it was unfair of the U.S. Chamber of Commerce and several other business groups to generate canned editorials to help defeat labor-law reform in Congress. And Ralph Nader argues it was unfair of the U.S. Chamber, the Business Roundtable, and other groups to blitz newspapers with canned editorials, columns, and cartoons to help defeat legislation to establish a federal Consumer Protection Agency.

In addition to disseminating canned editorials against these and other measures, the U.S. Chamber of Commerce has gathered editorials from hundreds of newspapers, including identically worded Chamber-originated editorials, and distributed them to lawmakers in an effort to show widespread grassroots support for the Chamber's positions. This, too, strikes critics as not cricket.

Indeed, the critics charge that much business advocacy has degenerated into media manipulation and has debased debate over policy alternatives. Mark Green, former director of Congress Watch, a Nader-founded group, thinks some business advocates don't play fair even in open debate. When Green debated U.S. Chamber President Richard Lesher on a Washington television station, Lesher, in a vein reminiscent of the red-baiting Senator Joseph R. McCarthy, accused Green of being "associated with a lot of socialists. Do you deny that?"

Whether or not Green, Rhoda Karpatkin of Consumers Union, and other business critics are correct that business advocacy is dangerously overwhelming opposing viewpoints, there is no question that it has unbalanced debate over specific issues. Smoking provides a case in point. Over the years the tobacco industry has spent billions of dollars to promote smoking as pleasurable, smart, and sexy. And in California, it has spent millions to twice defeat ballot measures calling for separate smoking and no-smoking sections in public places and work places. The $6.5 million that cigarette manufacturers poured in to help defeat Proposition 5 in 1978 was 10 times what the measure's backers could muster. And 1980's Proposition 10 was similarly "drowned in a sea of money," as its cash-short proponents put it.

As the smoking issue makes clear, in the marketplace of ideas, as at the ballot box, business more than holds its own.

10

Media Criticism
Helps Business

The remarkable thing about the business-press issue
is that it ever became an issue. Considering the generally neutral-to-sympathetic coverage the news
media have given business all along, it is surprising
that any businessmen thought to make a public
issue of press performance and thereby invite examination of the entire subject of business-media
relations.

It's true there was some provocation, notably
some network television news coverage that oversimplified complex issues, overplayed conflict and
even demonstrated an adversarial attitude toward
business. And too many newspapers, skimping on
space and staff for business news, threw ill-informed
and sometimes unsympathetic generalists into difficult business stories they could hardly avoid mud-
dling up.

But business's attack against the news media
seems to have been mainly an overreaction to negative news of corporate malfeasance, as disclosed by
government investigators, and to business's growing

unpopularity with the public, as disclosed by public opinion polls. Instead of taking positive steps to overcome the public's perception of business as too often unethical, profit-driven, and insensitive to consumers, the environment, and their own employees' health, some business leaders attempted to shift the blame to journalists and their presumed antibusiness bias. Instead of looking to the bad apples in business's own barrel, these businessmen pointed to the news media's barrel as tainted.

However, as this extensive examination of business–media relations has documented, what businessmen have labeled antibusiness bias usually turns out to be nothing more sinister than journalists doing their job—imperfectly, to be sure, but well within the standards that have made the American news media among the world's most professional. Simplistic, superficial, scattershot coverage—all too common. Deliberately distorted, hostile, antibusiness coverage—relatively rare.

What's more, the considerable volume of corporate advocacy and promotional fluff that business manages to get into print and on the air tends to offset coverage that puts business in a negative light. Business's case against the media might be more convincing if it acknowledged this, as well as the general support for business positions that newspaper editorials provide.

Even coverage that puts business in a bad light can be beneficial. Consumer affairs journalism provides a case in point. In making sure that businessmen deliver what they promise, consumer affairs journalists help cleanse the marketplace and protect reputable businessmen from unscrupulous competitors. Of course, this does not excuse consumer affairs journalists from allowing sympathy for consumerist positions to unbalance their reports or deny businessmen their say. Nor for advocating when they should simply be laying out the facts. Nor for playing on populist antibusiness sentiment to win ratings points.

Similarly, investigative reporters have no business badgering businessmen and stacking the deck against them, as some have done on network television, probably less from antibusiness bias than to make their stories seem important and airworthy. Competition for scarce time on the evening news isn't always good for either business or journalism.

The business-press issue has served a useful purpose in calling attention to weaknesses and excesses on both sides. Improvement is already detectable. Businessmen are showing more willingness to cooperate and be candid with journalists. And journalists seem less apt to go off half-cocked. Plenty of room for further improvement remains, however. Businessmen need to continue to open up and accommodate to stepped-up coverage of business and the economy. Journalists need to continue to improve the accuracy, fairness, and relevancy of their reports.

As the controversies affecting business grow increasingly technical, the news media need better trained specialists to report with sophistication on such intricate questions as industry's role in causing environmental damage and production workers' health problems. And as inflation, unemployment, and underutilized productive capacity persist, the news media need to assign more reporters to probe

the fundamental structure of the economy and of
individual industries, to see if built-in flaws are
causing problems.

Television bears a special responsibility because
of its huge audiences and its rent-free use of the
public airwaves for private profit. The least the TV
networks can do is to institute the equivalent of a
newspaper letters column by providing a format on
their newscasts for a minute or two of unedited
comment and rebuttal—not just by corporations,
but by environmentalists, consumerists and other
corporate critics as well.

Both business and the media need to recognize
that the nation needs the early warning system that
an alert media can provide in calling attention to
business practices and structural weaknesses that
require corrective action. Both, for instance, have
a powerful self-interest in the preservation of the
environment, on which their own long-range prosperity ultimately depends. And both have a powerful self-interest in the correction of abuses that pre-
vent the economy from working well.

Business and the news media must also recognize
that some tension, even conflict, is inherent in
business-media relations. Expecting total harmony
between the two is as undesirable as it is unrealis-
tic. In a pluralistic society, business and the media
serve different functions. Business produces goods
and services and provides jobs. The media have a
public responsibility to make sure that business
acts responsibly. The bottom line for business,
then, is that its own long-run self-interest, as well
as the nation's, depends on keeping the media
watchdog alert and on a long leash.

Bibliography

Allen, Frank. "News Releases from Business Irritate Editors." *The Wall Street Journal,* May 20, 1981.

Aronoff, Craig E., ed. *Business and the Media.* Santa Monica, Calif.: Goodyear Publishing, 1979.

Astor, Gerald. "The Gospel According to Mobil." [*MORE*], April 1976.

Baldwin, Deborah. "Ad Council Prescription: Public Service Pablum." *Washington Journalism Review,* October 1977.

_____. "*Harper's* War on Environmentalism." *Environmental Action,* October 21, 1978.

_____. "The Ads You Love to Hate." *Environmental Action,* September 1980.

Banks, Louis. "The Failings of Business and Journalism." *Time,* February 9, 1976.

_____. "Memo to the Press: They Hate You Out There." *Atlantic Monthly,* April 1978.

Barrett, Marvin. *Rich News, Poor News.* New York: Thomas Y. Crowell, 1978.

Beck, Robert A. "Business and the Media: Mutual Dilemmas Create Tension." *Dun's Review,* December 1978.

"Big Business on a Soapbox." *Marketing & Media Decisions,* June 1979.

Black, Jonathan. "The Stung" (On CBS's "60 Minutes").
Channels of Communications, April/May 1981.

Blodgett, Richard. "The Negative Business Press." *Corporate Communications Report,* July 1975.

Bonafede, Dom. "The Bull Market in Business/Economics Reporting." *Washington Journalism Review,* July/August 1980.

Buchanan, Patrick. "Journalism and Business: Scorpions in a Bottle." *TV Guide,* August 13, 1977.

Califano, Joseph A., Jr., and Howard Simons, eds. *The Media and Business.* New York: Random House, Vintage Books, 1979.

Cloherty, Jack. "Seven Flacks for Seven Sisters." *Washington Journalism Review,* January/February 1978.

Cooney, John E. "Does Business Want a Sophisticated Press or a Favorable One?" *The Wall Street Journal,* July 21, 1977.

Cordtz, Dan. "Businessmen Can Look Better if They Try." *New York Times,* July 18, 1976.

Culhane, John. "Where TV Documentaries Don't Dare to Tread." *New York Times,* February 20, 1977.

Cutlip, Scott M. "The Media and the Corporation: A Matter of Perception and Performance." In *Business and the Media,* edited by Craig E. Aronoff. Santa Monica, Calif.: Goodyear Publishing, 1979.

Dennis, Lloyd B. "Business Must Shoulder the Blame for Its Poor Image with Public and Press." *Los Angeles Times,* February 5, 1978.

Devereux, Sean. "Boosters in the Newsroom: The Jacksonville Case." *Columbia Journalism Review,* January/February 1976.

Diamond, Edwin. "Is TV Out to Get Big Oil?" *TV Guide,* May 17, 1980.

Diamond, Edwin, and Leigh Passman. "Three Mile Island: How Clear Was TV's Picture?" *TV Guide,* August 4, 1979.

Ferguson, James L. "Business and the News Media: Can We Find a Better Channel?" Address to Association of National Advertisers, October 14, 1976. Excerpted as

"Truth in Business News" in *New York Times,* December 10, 1976.

Finn, David. "Why Business Has Trouble with the Media, and Vice Versa." *Across the Board,* February 1978.

_____. "Mistrust: The Media-Business Syndrome." *Across the Board,* July 1979.

_____. *The Business-Media Relationship: Countering Misconceptions and Distrust.* New York: American Management Association, 1981.

Foryst, Carole. "Corporate Profits Up? 44%, 26% or . . ." *Washington Journalism Review,* June/July 1979.

Friedman, Robert. "Try American Capitalism Today!" (On the Advertising Council). *[MORE]*, May 1976.

Gannon, James P. Untitled address on business and the media at Drake University, October 24, 1979.

Gans, Herbert J. *Deciding What's News.* New York: Random House, 1979.

_____. "Is TV News Biased against Business?" *TV Guide,* July 5, 1980.

General Motors Corporation. *Business and the News Media—What Are the Roles of Each?* Summary of submissions to the 1979 General Motors Intercollegiate Business Understanding Program. Detroit: General Motors Corporation, 1979.

Gloede, W. F. "Editors Complain about Ad Department Takeover of Real Estate Section." *Editor & Publisher,* June 9, 1979.

Graham, Sandy. "Illinois Power Pans '60 Minutes'." *The Wall Street Journal,* June 27, 1980.

Green, Mark. "How Business Sways the Media." In *Business and the Media,* edited by Craig E. Aronoff. Santa Monica, Calif.: Goodyear Publishing, 1979.

Griffith, Thomas. "Must Business Fight the Press?" *Fortune,* June 1974.

Hall, Bob. "The Brown-Lung Controversy. How the Press, North and South, Handled a Story Involving the South's Largest Industry." *Columbia Journalism Review,* March/April 1978.

Henry, J. S. "From Soap to Soapbox: The Corporate Merchandising of Ideas." *Working Papers for a New Society,* May/June 1980.

Hubbard, J. T. W. "Business News in Post-Watergate Era." *Journalism Quarterly,* Autumn 1976.

Jasen, Georgette. "Chemical Industry Polishes Its Image in Drive to Combat Negative Publicity." *The Wall Street Journal,* September 11, 1980.

Karp, Richard. "Newspaper Food Pages: Credibility for Sale." *Columbia Journalism Review,* November/December 1971.

Kiester, Edwin, Jr. "That 'News' Item May Be a Commercial." *TV Guide,* October 5, 1974.

Kirkland, Lane. "Labor and the Press." *American Federationist,* December 1975.

Klein, Frederick C. "The Press's Cozy Relationship with Sports." *The Wall Street Journal,* June 26, 1979.

Klein, Jeffrey. "Semi-Tough: The Politics Behind '60 Minutes'." *Mother Jones,* September/October 1979.

Knopf, Terry Ann. "Plugola: What the Talk Shows Don't Talk About." *Columbia Journalism Review,* January/February 1977.

Kopkind, Andrew. "The Unwritten Watergate Story." *[MORE],* November 1974.

Kristol, Irving. "The Press and Business: An Adversary Relationship?" Address at University of California at Los Angeles, November 30, 1976.

Kuhn, Ferdinand. "Blighted Areas of Our Press." *Columbia Journalism Review,* Summer 1966.

Lawrence, John F. "The Press: Too Soft on Business?" In *Business and the Media,* edited by Craig E. Aronoff. Santa Monica, Calif.: Goodyear Publishing, 1979.

————. "Business-Media Debate: The Issues Need to be Put in Focus." *Los Angeles Times,* March 11, 1979.

————. "Business Can Improve Poor Image with a Few Basic Changes." *Los Angeles Times,* August 12, 1979.

————. "The Media Need Greater Commitment to Cover Business Fairly." *Los Angeles Times,* August 19, 1979.

Livingston, J. A. "Business and the Press: A Plea for Understanding." *Philadelphia Inquirer*, June 16, 1976.

McCartney, Laton. "How IBM Spindles the Media." [*MORE*], September 1973.

McClintick, David. "The Business Beat: Nation's Press Devotes More Space, Manpower to Economic Coverage." *The Wall Street Journal*, December 8, 1978.

McDowell, Edwin. "Bridging the Communications Gap." *Saturday Review*, September 29, 1979.

MacNaughton, Donald S. "Business and the Press—Independent or Interdependent?" Address to American Life Insurance Association and Institute of Life Insurance, November 4, 1975. Excerpted as "The Businessman versus the Journalist" in *New York Times*, March 7, 1976.

McPhatter, William, ed. *The Business Beat: Its Impact and Its Problems.* Indianapolis: Bobbs-Merrill, 1980.

Mahoney, David J. "On Ending an Adversary Relationship." *New York Times*, July 7, 1977.

Matthews, Leonard S. "1984: Here Already?" Address to American Association of Advertising Agencies, November 14, 1979.

Maxwell, Neil. "Health Issue: How Johns-Manville Mounts Counterattack in Asbestos Dispute." *The Wall Street Journal*, June 30, 1980.

Meadows, Edward. "Why the Oil Companies Are Coming Up Dry in Their Public Relations." *Fortune*, July 30, 1979.

Media Institute. *Television Evening News Covers Nuclear Energy: A Ten Year Perspective.* Washington, D.C.: Media Institute, 1979.

_____. *Punch, Counterpunch: "60 Minutes" vs. Illinois Power.* Washington, D.C.: Media Institute, 1981.

Milletti, Mario A. "Business Reporting Is Getting Better." *Corporate Communications Report*, November 1980.

Morris, Roger. "A Bullish Pulpit: The *New York Times*'s Business Desk." *Columbia Journalism Review*, May/June 1981.

National News Council. "Complaint No. 25: Mobil Oil Corporation against ABC-TV." Decided May 10, 1974.

————. "Complaint No. 117: Cohen et al. against NBC News." Decided November 15, 1977.

————. "Freedom of the Press Complaint: *The Day* against Electric Boat." Decided June 12, 1979.

————. "Complaint No. 169. Shell Oil Company against NBC News." Decided November 30, 1979.

————. "Complaint No. 172: Exxon Corporation against NBC News." Decided March 6, 1980.

————. "Complaint No. 184: The Association of American Railroads against ABC News." Decided March 6, 1981.

Otwell, Ralph. "Big, Bad Business in the Hands of the Devil Press." *The Quill,* April 1977.

Paletz, David L.; Roberta E. Pearson; and Donald L. Willis. *Politics in Public Service Advertising on Television.* New York: Praeger Publishers, 1977.

Phillips, Kevin P. "Why Many People Are Turning against the Media." *Enterprise,* May 1978.

Poe, Randall. "Masters of the Advertorial: Mobil's Extraordinary Advocacy Advertising Campaign Is Still Making Tall Waves." *Across the Board,* September 1980.

Poindexter, Joseph. "The Great Industry-Media Debate." *Saturday Review,* July 10, 1976.

Pollock, Francis. "The National Chicken Cooking Contest: How to Get Finger-Lickin'-Good Coverage from the U.S. Press." *Columbia Journalism Review,* November/December 1975.

————. "Newspaper Food Sections: The Palate's Guard or Food Industry Flackery?" *Washington Journalism Review,* October 1980.

Radolf, Andrew. "Big City Dailies Expand Business News Coverage." *Editor & Publisher,* June 7, 1980.

Ridgeway, James. "Trying to Catch the Energy Crisis." [*MORE*], January 1974.

Roalman, Arthur R. "Stock Tables—A Waste?" *Editor & Publisher,* December 14, 1974.

Ross, Irwin. "Public Relations Isn't Kid-Glove Stuff at Mobil." *Fortune,* September 1976.

Rubin, Bernard et al. *Big Business and the Mass Media.* Lexington, Mass.: D. C. Heath, Lexington Books, 1977.

Rubin, David M., and David P. Sachs. *Mass Media and the Environment: Water Resources, Land Use and Atomic Energy in California.* New York: Praeger Publishers, 1973.

Rubin, Gail, and Peter Maier. *For Sale or Rent: A Critical Study of Newspaper Real Estate Sections.* Washington, D.C.: Housing Research Group, 1978.

Saltzman, Joe. "Newscasters as Pitchmen: A Question of Credibility?" *Los Angeles Times,* October 29, 1978.

Samuelson, Robert J. "The Oil Companies and the Press." *Columbia Journalism Review,* January/February 1974.

Sandman, Peter M., and Mary Paden. "At Three Mile Island." *Columbia Journalism Review,* July/August, 1979.

Sansweet, Stephen J. "Arco TV Show Combats 'Bias' of Newscasts." *The Wall Street Journal,* August 1, 1980.

Schmertz, Herbert. "Idea Advertising: Talking to New Audiences." *Electric Perspectives,* June 1976.

————. "An Energy Story the Press Hasn't Told." *Fortune,* November 5, 1979.

Sesser, Stanford N. "The Fantasy World of Travel Sections." *Columbia Journalism Review,* Spring 1970.

Sethi, S. Prakash. *Advocacy Advertising and Large Corporations.* Lexington, Mass.: D. C. Heath, Lexington Books, 1977.

————. "Grassroots Lobbying and the Corporation." *Business & Society Review,* Spring 1979.

Sethi, S. Prakash, and Herbert Schmertz. "Industry Fights Back: The Debate over Advocacy Advertising." *Saturday Review,* January 21, 1978.

Shapley, Deborah. "Reporting on Nuclear Power: The Tennessee Valley Case." *Columbia Journalism Review,* March/April 1977.

Silk, Leonard, and David Vogel. *Ethics and Profits: The Crisis of Confidence in American Business.* New York: Simon & Schuster, 1976.

Sleeper, David. "Do the Media Too Often Miss the Message?" *Conservation Foundation Letter,* January 1979.

Smith, Lee. "Oil Meets the Press." *Dun's Review,* April 1974.

————. "Business and the Media." *Dun's Review,* March 1976.

Surface, Bill. "The Shame of the Sports Beat." *Columbia Journalism Review,* January/February 1972.

Tavoulareas, William P. "Freedom of the Press—License to Hurt?" *Saturday Review,* April 28, 1979.

Taylor, Arthur R. "Business and the Press: Who's Doing What to Whom and Why?" Address to Financial Executives Institute, October 21, 1975.

Vogel, David. "Business's 'New Class' Struggle." *The Nation,* December 15, 1979.

Weaver, Paul H. "Business/Journalism Freeze Shows Signs of Thaw." *Enterprise,* March 1981.

Weiss, Eric A. "The Public—Business's Ally or Adversary?" Address to Association of National Advertisers, November 29, 1977.

Welles, Chris. "The Bleak Wasteland of Financial Journalism." *Columbia Journalism Review,* July/August 1973.

————. "Business Journalism's Glittering Prizes." *Columbia Journalism Review,* March/April 1979.

West, Frederic W., Jr. "Economic and Business Reporting: Its Strengths and Weaknesses." Address to American Newspaper Publishers Association, May 4, 1976.

"What Newspapers Say About Real Estate—Can You Believe It?" *Changing Times,* February 1980.

Wriston, Walter B. "Alarm Is the Order of the Day." *[MORE]*, May 1976.

Young, Lewis H. "Business and the Media: The Failure to Understand How the Other Operates." *Vital Speeches,* November 15, 1978.

Index

149